P9-CKX-133

DATE DUE

DEMCO 38-296

MALCOLM ARNOLD

Sir Malcolm Arnold
(from a painting by Marialuisa Marino, courtesy of the artist)

MALCOLM ARNOLD
A Bio-Bibliography

STEWART R. CRAGGS

Bio-Bibliographies in Music, Number 69
Donald L. Hixon, *Series Adviser*

GREENWOOD PRESS
Westport, Connecticut • London

Riverside Community College
'00   Library
MAY   4800 Magnolia Avenue
Riverside, CA 92506

ML 134 .A77 C73 1998

Craggs, Stewart R.

Malcolm Arnold

Library of Congress Cataloging-in-Publication Data

Craggs, Stewart R.
    Malcolm Arnold : a bio-bibliography / Stewart R. Craggs.
       p.   cm.—(Bio-bibliographies in music, ISSN 0742-6968 ; no.
69)
    Includes discography (p.), bibliographical references (p.),
and index.
    ISBN 0-313-29254-X (alk. paper)
    1. Arnold, Malcolm—Bibliography. 2. Arnold, Malcolm—
Discography. I. Title. II. Series.
ML134.A77C73   1998
780′.92—dc21   98-28639
            MN

British Library Cataloguing in Publication Data is available.

Copyright © 1998 by Stewart R. Craggs

All rights reserved. No portion of this book may be
reproduced, by any process or technique, without the
express written consent of the publisher.

Library of Congress Catalog Card Number: 98-28639
ISBN: 0-313-29254-X
ISSN: 0742-6968

First published in 1998

Greenwood Press, 88 Post Road West, Westport, CT 06881
An imprint of Greenwood Publishing Group, Inc.

Printed in the United States of America

The paper used in this book complies with the
Permanent Paper Standard issued by the National
Information Standards Organization (Z39.48–1984).

10 9 8 7 6 5 4 3 2 1

Dedicated to
the memory
of

Kenneth Brian Swallow
(12 September 1931 - 22 February 1992)

Friend and mentor

Contents

Preface

Sir Malcolm Arnold is one of Britain's most distinguished, versatile and prolific twentieth century composers, his music ranging across a wide spectrum of forms from opera and ballet through orchestral and chamber music to film and incidental music. He is therefore a most appropriate subject for the Greenwood Press composer bio-bibliography series.

The present volume (the result of over ten years of research) attempts to document his vast and varied output, and is intended as a guide to resources for those wishing to undertake further research.

It consists of the following:

1)   a very brief <u>biography</u> of Sir Malcolm Arnold. This is intended merely to provide a broad outline of the composer's life. The first authorised biography of Sir Malcolm was published in 1994 and written by Piers Burton-Page (see B117). Others are currently being written or planned.

2)   a list and details of <u>works and performances</u>, classified by genre and then arranged alphabetically by title of composition. Each work is prefaced by the mnemonic "W."

3)   a select <u>discography</u> of recently released recordings, all commercially produced on compact disc. Each is listed alphabetically by title and each prefaced by the mnemonic "D."

4)   an annotated <u>bibliography</u> of writings by and about Sir Malcolm Arnold, his style and music. Each is prefaced by the mnemonic

"B." Entries in this section refer to "Works and Performances" and "Discography."

In addition, appendices provide alphabetical and chronological listings of Arnold's works. A complete general <u>index</u> concludes the volume.

Acknowledgements

My grateful thanks must be recorded to Anthony J. Day for his help, generosity and kindness to me in the preparation of this volume. It has, over the years, been a joy and a privilege to visit Sir Malcolm and Anthony at their home in Attleborough (Norfolk). Much of my work would not have been completed without their valuable guidance and assistance.

Amongst others who have helped over the years are Christopher Bornet (Royal College of Music Library), Professor John C. Dressler (Music Dept, Murray State University), Marialuisa Marino for very kindly supplying me with a copy of her painting of Sir Malcolm to use as a frontispiece, Colin Merton, Librarian of the Savile Club, London, Fiona Southey (Promotion Department, Novello & Co. Ltd.), Jan Thompson for producing a magnificently typed manuscript, Arline Usden, editor of *The Lady* and Keith Wilson (Director of the International Media Centre at the University of Salford).

Last, but not least, I must thank Valerie, my wife, for her valuable support throughout the preparation of this volume.

BIOGRAPHY

Malcolm Henry Arnold

Malcolm Henry Arnold was born on 21 October 1921 in Northampton, the youngest child of William and Annie Arnold.

Annie Arnold was a descendent of William Hawes, and she inherited the family's strong musical instincts. Hawes (1785-1846) has been a prominent figure in London musical life, holding appointments at Westminster Abbey and St. Paul's Cathedral. Arnold remembers his mother as a very accomplished pianist and accompanist, and she played a very important part in his early musical education.

Malcolm was closer to his sister, Ruth, than to Philip, his immediate elder brother. When Philip, who had joined the R.A.F., was shot down and killed in a raid over Berlin, the loss was a devastating blow to the whole family. It also resulted in Malcolm and his mother drawing closer in his early years: see the dedications of some of the early compositions, usually birthday presents.

He always said that he wanted to compose, ever since he was a child, and so it was arranged for Malcolm to have lessons from Philip Pfaff, organist at St. Matthew's Church in Northampton. Pfaff provided him with foundations in harmony and counterpoint that were to serve him well in his future career.

Jazz was another passion, and for his sixteenth birthday in 1937 he received an expensive high Bach trumpet. He had had lessons from the age of twelve, again with his mother advising and encouraging. Three years later he was able to travel to London for private lessons with Ernest Hall, the celebrated trumpet player. It was also in 1937 that Malcolm won a scholarship to the Royal College of Music where Hall was Professor.

His first tutor in composition was Patrick Hadley, a minor English composer, and then the more prolific composer Gordon Jacob, a pupil of C.V. Stanford. Trumpet lessons also continued and at Easter 1937, Malcolm undertook his first professional trumpet engagements in Llandudno, North Wales.

Before the conclusion of his second year at the Royal College, Arnold was offered - and accepted - the position of second trumpet in the London Philharmonic Orchestra. He left the College without any formal qualification, although he was made a fellow many years later. Malcolm was therefore able to learn much from sitting in an orchestra and being directed by some of the greatest conductors of the day - Anatole Fistoulari, Edward van Beinum, Bruno Walter, Ernest Ansermet and Adrian Boult to name but a few. Within a year, Malcolm Arnold, at the age of 21, found himself as Principal Trumpet of the L.P.O.

At the beginning of World War II, Arnold was registered as a conscientious objector, on condition that he pursued his musical activities. Later, he was to reverse this decision and he volunteered for the Buffs and underwent full military training. At the end of the war, Arnold resumed his position as first trumpet with the L.P.O. and stayed there until 1948 when an early composition, the overture *Beckus the Dandipratt* (W12) written in 1943, was recorded by the orchestra for the Decca Recording Company. It was the first of his works to win him widespread recognition.

It was also in 1948 that the Royal College awarded Arnold the Mendelssohn Scholarship, a travelling bursary which enabled him, on the advice of Sir George Dyson (Principal of the Royal College), to spend several months in Italy composing.

After his return from Italy, Arnold gradually turned to full-time composition, concentrating on his *First Symphony* (W67) which was completed on 11th February 1949. Running parallel was Arnold's work as a film composer; his natural fluency and ability providing him with fame and fortune for the next twenty years. His most famous film score was *The Bridge on the River Kwai* (W172) for which he received an Oscar (1957).

The 1950s saw the completion of two further symphonies and numerous concertos, together with many shorter pieces. Arnold was commissioned in 1953 for *Homage to the Queen* (W6), a ballet celebrating the coronation of Queen Elizabeth II. Two further one-act ballets were also composed and performed by the Royal Ballet.

By the middle of the 1960s, Malcolm Arnold decided that he had enough of London musical life and went to live in Cornwall with his second wife, Isobel. Important works which date from this time include the *Four Cornish Dances* (W41), *The Padstow Lifeboat* (W308), a march for brass and the overture,

Peterloo (W51), commissioned by the Trades Union Congress.

In 1972, Arnold left Cornwall and went to live in Ireland, settling just outside the city of Dublin. It was during this period that the *Seventh Symphony* (W73) was finished on 9 September 1973. The composer described the Symphony as a 'loose musical portrait' of his three children, Katherine, Robert and Edward, to whom the work is dedicated. The *Fantasy on a Theme of John Field for Piano and Orchestra* (W38), and the *Second String Quartet* of 1975 (W114) are two other important Dublin works.

The following year, the year of the American bicentennial, Arnold renewed his links with the U.S.A. He was asked to write a work for his old orchestra, the London Philharmonic, which was making a bicentennial tour, and he responded with the *Philharmonic Concerto* (W52), a work full of vitality and zest. Another work which has American connections, and which was started in Dublin but completed on his return to London, is the *Eighth Symphony* (W74). It was premiered at Albany by the Albany Symphony Orchestra, and the first British performance was given in 1981.

After these works and the *Symphony for Brass* (W314), nothing further was written because of personal problems (except for the *Trumpet Concerto* (W27) of 1982), until 1986 when he went to live in East Anglia. When Arnold came to Norfolk, his doctors gave him two years to live and predicted he would never compose again. His recovery, mostly due to the care and encouragement of Anthony John Day over the years, can only be described as a miracle. Arnold completed his *Ninth Symphony* (W75) in September 1986 and dedicated it to Day. Other works he was able to write include a *Fantasy for Recorder* (W99) and a *Fantasy for Cello* (W92). He retired from composition however in 1991, and was knighted by the Queen in 1993 for his services to English music. The year 1996 marked his 75th birthday with many celebrations.

WORKS AND
PERFORMANCES

I.   OPERAS

W1.   *THE DANCING MASTER* (Opus 34 - 1952)
       Opera in one act
       Libretto by Joe Mendoza, after a play by William Wycherley
       6 singers/1+1.2.2.2/4.3.3.1/timpani percussion celesta harp/ strings

       Duration: 55 minutes
       First performance: Barnes (London), Music Club (Kitson Hall), 1
       March 1962. Soloists with piano reduction of orchestra parts
       Unpublished
       SEE: B122, B182

W2.   *HENRI CHRISTOPHE*: 1949 (unfinished)
       Opera with libretto by Joe Mendoza
       4 singers/3.2.2.2/4.3.3.1/timpani percussion (2) harp/strings

       The opera was intended for the Festival of Britain, 1951, but was turned
       down on submission of the draft

W3.   *THE OPEN WINDOW* (Opus 56 - 1956)
       Opera in one act
       Libretto by Sidney Gilliat, after a short story by Saki
       6 singers/1.0.1.1/1.0.0.0/percussion harp/2vn va vc db

       Duration: 21½ minutes
       First performance: London, BBC Television, 14 December 1956.
            Soloists with the English Opera Group

Orchestra conducted by Lionel Salter
Unpublished
SEE: B123, B311

W4.   *UP AT THE VILLA*: 1951? (Unfinished)
Opera in one act
Libretto after Robert Browning

Joe Mendoza drafted a synopsis that formed the basis of Arnold's own
libretto.
Arnold made preliminary sketches, but subsequently destroyed them.

II.   BALLETS

W5.   *ELECTRA* (Opus 79 - 1963)
Ballet in one act. Choreography by Robert Helpmann

Commissioned by: The Royal Ballet
2+1.2.2.2/4.3.3.1/timpani percussion (3) harp/strings
Duration: 25 minutes
First performance: London, Royal Opera House, Covent Garden, 26
March 1963. Dancers of the Royal Ballet with the orchestra of the Royal
Opera House, Covent Garden, conducted by John Lanchberry
Unpublished
See: B112

W6.   *HOMAGE TO THE QUEEN* (Opus 42 - 1953)
Ballet with choreography by Frederick Ashton

Commissioned to celebrate the Coronation of HM Queen Elizabeth II
2+1.2.2.2/4.3.3.1/timpani percussion (2) celesta harp/strings
Duration: 40 minutes
First performance: London, Royal Opera House, Covent Garden, 2 June
        1953.   Dancers of the Sadler's Wells Theatre Ballet with the
        orchestra of the Royal Opera House, Covent Garden, conducted by
        Robert Irving
First USA: New York, Metropolitan Opera House, September 1953
Publication: Paterson, 1953
RECORDING: D43
SEE: B213, B370

OTHER VERSIONS
(1) HOMAGE TO THE QUEEN: ballet suite (Opus 42a)
for orchestra

2+1.2.2.2/4.3.3.1/timpani percussion (2) celesta harp/strings
Duration: 17 minutes
First performance: Northampton, New Theatre, 19 July 1953.
    London Philharmonic Orchestra, conducted by Malcolm Arnold
Unpublished

(2) HOMAGE TO THE QUEEN: suite for piano solo (Opus 42b)

Duration: 9 minutes
Publication: Paterson, 1954
RECORDING: D43

W7.   *RINALDO AND ARMIDA* (Opus 49): 1954
       Ballet with choreography by Frederick Ashton

       2+1.2.2.2/4.3.3.1/timpani percussion (2) celesta harp/strings
       Duration: 23 minutes
       First performance: London, Royal Opera House, Covent Garden, 6
       January 1955. Dancers of the Sadler's Wells Theatre Ballet with the
       orchestra of the Royal Opera House, Covent Garden, conducted by
       Malcolm Arnold.
       Unpublished
       SEE: B370

W8.   *SOLITAIRE:* 1956
       Ballet with choreography by Kenneth MacMillan

       The music for Solitaire comprises the two sets of English Dances (W34
       and W35), together with two newly composed dances, Sarabande and
       Polka

       2+1.2.2.2/4.3.3.1/timpani percussion (2) celesta harp/strings
       Duration: 25½ minutes
       First performance: London, Sadler's Wells Theatre, 7 June 1956.
           Dancers of the Sadler's Wells Theatre Ballet with the Sadler's
           Wells Theatre Orchestra, conducted by John Lanchberry
       Publication: Paterson, 1956
       RECORDING: D58

OTHER VERSIONS
(1) Solitaire: Sarabande and Polka (only) arranged for piano solo
Publication: Paterson, 1959

(2) Solitaire: Sarabande and Polka (only) arranged for symphonic wind
band by John Paynter
Publication: Paterson and Carl Fischer, 1983

W9.   *SWEENEY TODD* (Opus 68 - 1959)
Ballet with choreography by John Cranko

1+1.1.2.1/2.2.2.0/timpani percussion piano celesta harp/strings
Duration: 23 minutes
First performance: Stratford upon Avon, Shakespeare Memorial Theatre,
10 December 1959. Dancers of the Royal Ballet with the orchestra of
the Royal Opera House, Covent Garden, conducted by John Lanchberry
First London: Royal Opera House, Covent Garden, 26 August 1960
Unpublished
See: B99, B315

OTHER VERSIONS
(1) Sweeney Todd: concert suite for orchestra (Opus 68a)
1+1.1.2.1/2.2.2.0/timpani percussion piano celesta harp/strings
Duration: 12 minutes
This concerts site was drawn from the complete ballet score in 1984 by
David Ellis in association with the composer
Publication: Faber, 1984
RECORDING: D69

W10.   *THE THREE MUSKETEERS:* 1976

Sketches (short score) of a ballet held by the Royal College of Music,
London

III.   ORCHESTRAL MUSIC

W11.   *ANNIVERSARY OVERTURE* (Opus 99 - 1968)
for orchestra

Written for the 21st anniversary (originally titled *Hong Kong
Anniversary Overture)* of the founding of the Hong Kong Philharmonic

Society
2.2.2.2/4.2.3.0/timpani percussion/strings
Duration: 4 minutes
First performance: Hong Kong, City Hall, 8 December 1968.
    Hong Kong Philharmonic Orchestra, conducted by Arrigo Foa
First British: London Royal Festival Hall, 17 September 1970.
    Light Music Society Orchestra, conducted by Malcolm Arnold
Publication: Faber Music, 1974 (in conjunction with the Central Music
        Library)

W12.   *BECKUS THE DANDIPRATT* (Opus 5 - 1943)
    Overture for orchestra

    2+1.2.2.2/4.2+cnt.3.1/timpani percussion/strings
    Duration: 8½ minutes
    First performance: Broadcast in the BBC Third Programme, 29
    November 1946. BBC Scottish Orchestra, conducted by Ian Whyte
    First Concert performance: London Royal Opera House, Covent Garden,
        16 November 1947. London Philharmonic Orchestra conducted by
        Edward van Beinum
    First USA: Illinois University Auditorium, 29 March 1952.
        University of Illinois Symphony Orchestra, conducted by Rafael
        Kubelik
    Publication: Lengnick, 1948
    RECORDING: D2
    SEE: B89

W13.   *CARNIVAL OF ANIMALS* (Opus 72 - 1960)
    for orchestra

    1 - The Giraffe (Allegretto)
    2 - Sheep (Poco lento)
    3 - Cows (Moderato)
    4 - Mice (Vivace)
    5 - Jumbo (Andante)
    6 - Chiroptera

    Commissioned for the Hoffnung Memorial Concert
    2+1.2.2.2/4.3.3.1/timpani percussion (2)/strings
    Duration: 15 minutes
    First performance: London, Royal Festival Hall, 31 October 1960.
        Morley College Symphony Orchestra, conducted by Malcolm
        Arnold

Unpublished
RECORDING: D4

W14.   *COMMONWEALTH CHRISTMAS OVERTURE* (Opus 64 - 1957)
for orchestra

Commissioned by the BBC for Christmas Round the World (1957),
marking the 25th anniversary of the first Christmas broadcast by a
British monarch
2+1.2.2.2/4.3.3.1/timpani percussion (4) celesta harp/strings (plus 3
guitars, marimba and an Afro-Cuban percussion group)
Duration: 14½ minutes
First broadcast performance: London, BBC Television, 25 December
     1957. BBC Symphony Orchestra, conducted by Rudolf Schwarz
Unpublished
RECORDING: D6

W15.   *CONCERTO [NO.1] FOR CLARINET AND STRINGS* (Opus 20 -
1948)

I   - Allegro
II   - Andante con moto
III   - Allegro con fuoco

Dedication: Frederick Thurston
Duration: 16½ minutes
First performance: Edinburgh, Usher Hall, 29 August 1949.
     Frederick Thurston (clarinet) with the Jacques Orchestra, conducted
     by Reginald Jacques
First USA: Los Angeles, Royce Hall (University of California), 2
     October 1967. Benny Goodman (clarinet) with the California
     Chamber Symphony Orchestra, conducted by Hendi Temianka
Publication: Lengnick, 1952
RECORDING: D8
SEE: B55, B231

W16.   *CONCERTO [NO.2] FOR CLARINET AND ORCHESTRA*
(Opus 115 -1974)

I   - Allegro vivace
II   - Lento
III   - Allegro non troppo - Prestissimo (The Pre-Goodman Rag)

1+ 1.2.0.2/2.0.0.0/timpani percussion/strings
Dedication: Benny Goodman 'with admiration and affection'
Duration: 17½ minutes
First performance: Red Rocks, Denver (Colorado), 17 August 1974.
    Benny Goodman (clarinet) and the Denver Symphony Orchestra,
    conducted by Brian Priestman
First British: London, St John's Smith Square, 11 October 1976.
    Benny Goodman (clarinet) and the Park Lane Music Players,
    conducted by Malcolm Arnold
Publication: Faber Music, 1981
RECORDING: D9
See: B71, B175, B364

W17.   *CONCERTO FOR FLUTE AND STRINGS* (Opus 45 - 1954)

    I   - Allegro energico
    II   - Andante
    III   - Con fuoco - Presto

Dedication: Richard Adeney [for whom it was written]
Duration: 12½ minutes
First performance: London, Victoria and Albert Museum, 11 April 1954.
    Richard Adeney (flute) with the Boyd Neel Orchestra, conducted by
    John Hollingsworth
Publication: Paterson, 1954
SEE: B60, B64, B66, B235, B245

W18.   *CONCERTO [NO.2] FOR FLUTE AND ORCHESTRA* (Opus 111 -
        1972)

    I   - Allegro moderato
    II   - Vivace
    III   - Allegretto

0.2.0.0/2.0.0.0/strings
Dedication: Richard Adeney
Duration: 14 minutes
First performance: Snape, The Maltings, 28 June 1973.
    Richard Adeney (flute) with the English Chamber Orchestra,
    conducted by Kenneth Sillito
First London: Queen Elizabeth Hall, 1 October 1973.
    Richard Adeney (flute) with the English Chamber Orchestra,
    conducted by Wilfred Boettcher

Publication: Faber Music, 1973
RECORDING: D10
SEE: W279, B377

W19.   *CONCERTO FOR GUITAR AND CHAMBER ORCHESTRA* (Opus 67
- 1959)

I   - Allegro
II   - Lento [dedicated to the memory of Django Reinhardt]
III   - Con brio

Commissioned by Julian Bream
1.0.1.0/1.0.0.0/vn va vc db
Dedication: Julian Bream
Duration: 21½ minutes
First performance: Broadcast in the BBC Third Programme, 18 June
       1959. Julian Bream (guitar) with the Melos Ensemble, conducted
       by Malcolm Arnold
First concert performance: Aldeburgh, Jubilee Hall, 25 June 1959.
       Julian Bream (guitar) with the Melos Ensemble, conducted by
       Malcolm Arnold
First London: Victoria and Albert Museum, 6 March 1960.
       Julian Bream (guitar) with the Melos Ensemble, conducted by
       Malcolm Arnold
Publication: Paterson, 1961
RECORDING: D11
SEE: B201

W20.   *CONCERTO AND HARMONICA AND ORCHESTRA* (Opus 46 - 1954)

I   - Grazioso
II   - Mesto
III   - Con brio - Presto

Commissioned by the BBC
0.0.0.0/4.3.3.1/timpani percussion (2)/strings
Dedication: Larry Adler [for whom it was written]
Duration: 9 minutes
First performance: London, Royal Albert Hall, 14 August 1954.
       Larry Adler (harmonica) and the BBC Symphony Orchestra,
       conducted by Malcolm Arnold
Publication: Peterson, 1954
SEE: B15, B309

W21.   *CONCERTO [NO.1] FOR HORN AND ORCHESTRA* (Opus 11 - 1945)

I   - Allegro commodo
II   - Andante con moto
III - Allegro con brio

2+1.2.2.2/0.0.0.0/timpani/strings
Dedication: Charles Gregory
Duration: 22 minutes
First performance: London, Royal Opera House, Covent Garden, 8
December 1946. Charles Gregory (horn) with the London Philharmonic
Orchestra, conducted by Ernest Ansermet
Publication: Lengnick, 1947
RECORDING: D12
SEE: B16

W22.   *CONCERTO [NO.2] FOR HORN AND STRINGS* (Opus 58 - 1956)

I   - Con energico
II   - Andante grazioso
III - Vivace - Presto

Dedication: Dennis Brain
Duration: 13½ minutes
First performance: Cheltenham, Town Hall, 17 July 1957.
    Dennis Brain (horn) with the Hallé Orchestra, conducted by
    Malcolm Arnold
Publication: Paterson, 1956
RECORDING: D13
SEE: B1, B222

W23.   *CONCERTO FOR OBOE AND STRINGS* (Opus 39 - 1952)

I   - Cantabile
II   - Vivace
III - Quasi allegretto - Lento - Vivace

Commissioned by Leon Goossens
Dedication: Leon Goossens
Duration: 15 minutes
First performance: London, Royal Festival Hall, 26 June 1953.

Leon Goossens (oboe) with the Boyd Neel Orchestra, conducted by Boyd Neel

Publication: Paterson, 1952

W24.   *CONCERTO FOR ORGAN AND ORCHESTRA* (Opus 47 - 1954)

I   - Vivace
II   - Lento
III - Allegretto

Written for Denis Vaughan and specially composed for the organ of the Royal Festival Hall, London

0.0.0.0/0.1+2.0.0/timpani/strings

Duration: 12½ minutes

First performance: London, Royal Festival Hall, 11 December 1954.
        Denis Vaughan (organ) with the London Symphony Orchestra, conducted by Leslie Woodgate

Publication: Paterson, 1954

W25.   *CONCERTO FOR PIANO DUET AND STRINGS* (Opus 32 - 1951)

I   - Allegro
II   - Larghetto - Allegretto - Larghetto
III - Vivace - Presto

Composed at the suggestion of Mosco Carner

Dedication: Helen Pyke and Paul Hamburger

Duration: 21½ minutes

First performance: Broadcast in the BBC Third Programme, 17 August 1951.
        Helen Pyke and Paul Hamburger (pianos) with the Goldsborough Orchestra, conducted by Mosco Carner

First London: Royal Albert Hall, 31 July 1953.
        Helen Pyke and Paul Hamburger (pianos) with the London Symphony Orchestra, conducted by Basil Cameron

Publication: Lengnick, 1951

RECORDING: D14

SEE: B318, B331

W26.   *CONCERTO FOR RECORDER [DESCANT/SOPRANINO] AND ORCHESTRA* (Opus 133 - 1988)

I   - Allegro
II   - Lento
III - Vivace

Commissioned by the English Sinfonia with funds provided by the Eastern Arts Association
0.2.0.0/2.0.0.0/strings
Dedication: For Michala Petri
Duration: 14 minutes
First performance: Parish Church of Eye, 3 June 1988.
    Michala Petri (recorder) with the English Sinfonia, conducted by Steuart Bedford
Publication: Faber Music, 1992
RECORDING: D15

W27. *CONCERTO FOR TRUMPET AND ORCHESTRA* (Opus 125 - 1982)

I   - Allegro energico
II   - Andante con moto
III - Vivace

Commissioned by the Arts Council of Great Britain in celebration of the 100th Anniversary of the founding of the Royal College of Music in 1883
2.2.2.2/4.2.3.1/timpani percussion (2) harp/strings
Duration: 11½ minutes
First performance: London, Royal Albert Hall, 30 January 1983.
    John Wallace (trumpet) with the RCM Great Gala Orchestra, conducted by Alexander Gibson
Publication: Faber Music, 1982
SEE: B73, B124, B197

W28. *CONCERTO FOR TWENTY-EIGHT PLAYERS* (Opus 105 - 1970)

I   - Vivace
II   - Larghetto
III - Allegro

Commissioned by the Stuyvesant Foundation
1.2.0.1/2.0.0.0/strings (6 6 4 4 2)
Duration: 15 minutes
First performance: London, Queen Elizabeth Hall, 25 April 1970.
    English Chamber Orchestra, conducted by Malcolm Arnold

Publication: Faber Music, 1970
RECORDING: D16
SEE: B95, B201

W29.   *CONCERTO FOR TWO PIANOS (3 HANDS) AND ORCHESTRA*
(Opus 104 - 1969)

I   - Allegro moderato
II   - Andante con moto
III - Allegro

Commissioned by the BBC
2+1.2.2..2/4.3.3.1/timpani percussion (2) harp/strings
Dedication: To Phyllis and Cyril with affection and admiration
Duration: 12½ minutes
First performance: London, Royal Albert Hall, 16 August 1969.
    Phyllis Sellick and Cyril Smith (pianos) with the BBC Symphony
    Orchestra, conducted by Malcolm Arnold
Publication: Faber Music, 1969
RECORDING: D17
SEE: B46, B134, B136, B320, B348, B372

W30.   *CONCERTO FOR TWO VIOLINS AND STRING ORCHESTRA*
(Opus 77 - 1962)

I   - Allegro risoluto
II   - Andantino
III - Vivace - Presto

Commissioned by Yehudi Menuhin
Duration: 16½ minutes
First performance: Bath, Guildhall, 24 June 1962.
    Yehudi Menuhin and Albert Lysy (violins) with the Bath Festival
    Orchestra, conducted by Malcolm Arnold
First London: Victoria and Albert Museum, 17 June 1964.
    Yehudi Menuhin and Robert Masters (violins) with the Bath
    Festival Orchestra, conducted by Malcolm Arnold
Publication: Faber Music. 1966
RECORDING: D18
SEE: B302, B341

W31.   *CONCERTO FOR VIOLA AND CHAMBER ORCHESTRA* (Opus 108 -
1971)

I   - Allegro con spirito
II   - Andante con moto
III   - Allegro vivace

Commissioned by Northern Arts
1.2.2.2/2.0.0.0/strings
Dedication: Roger Best and the Northern Sinfonia
Durations: 20 minutes
First performance: Carlisle, Market Hall, 13 October 1971.
  Roger Best (viola) with the Northern Sinfonia, conducted by
  Malcolm Arnold
First London: Queen Elizabeth Hall, 15 October 1971.
  Roger Best (viola) with the Northern Sinfonia, conducted by
  Malcolm Arnold
Publication: Faber Music, 1980
RECORDING: D19
SEE: B324, B383

W32.   *DIVERTIMENTO [NO.1] FOR ORCHESTRA* (Opus 1 - 1942)

I   - Moderato - Vivace
II   - Andante con modo (Chaconne) - Allegro

3.2.2.2/4.3.3.1/timpani percussion (2)/strings
Duration: 10½ minutes
First performance: London, Guildhall School of Music, 29 May 1945.
  London Symphony Orchestra, conducted by Benjamin Frankel
Unpublished

W33.   *DIVERTIMENTO [NO.2] FOR ORCHESTRA* (Opus 24 - 1950)

I   - Fanfare (Allegro)
II   - Tango (Lento)
III   - Chaconne (Allegro con spirito)

Written for the National Youth Orchestra of Great Britain
2+1.2.2.2/4.3.3.1/timpani percussion (2) harp/strings
Duration: 9 minutes
First performance: Brighton, The Dome, 19 April 1950.
  National Youth Orchestra of Great Britain, conducted by Reginald
  Jacques
First London: Royal Albert Hall, 10 August 1957.
  NYOGB, conducted by Hugo Rignold

SEE: B109, B344

OTHER VERSIONS
In 1961, Arnold completely re-worked the Divertimento which became
Opus 75, with the central movement retitled Nocturne (Lento)

First performance: Leeds, Town Hall, 24 October 1961.
    Royal Liverpool Philharmonic Orchestra, conducted by Lawrence
    Leonard
First London: Royal Festival Hall, 26 March 1962.
    Royal Philharmonic Orchestra, conducted by Kenneth Jones
Publication: Paterson, 1961
SEE: B36, B366

W34.   *ENGLISH DANCES [SET 1]* (Opus 27 - 1950)

    I   - Andantino
    II   - Vivace
    III   - Mesto
    IV   - Allegro risoluto

    2+1.2.2.2/4.3.3.1/timpani percussion (2) celesta harp/strings
    Dedication: Bernard de Nevers [Lengnick]
    Duration: 8 minutes
    First performance: London, Central Hall (East Ham), 14 April 1951.
        London Philharmonic Orchestra, conducted by Adrian Boult
    Publication: Lengnick, 1951
    RECORDING: D23
    See: B52

    OTHER VERSIONS
    (1) *English Dances (Set 1):* arranged for piano duet (Reizenstein)
    Publication: Lengnick, 1958

    (2) *English Dances (Set 1):* arranged for wind band (Johnstone)
    Publication: Lengnick, 1965

W35.   *ENGLISH DANCES [SET 2]* (Opus 33 - 1951)

    V   - Allegro non troppo
    VI   - Con brio
    VII - Grazioso

VIII- Giubiloso - Lento e maestoso

2+1.2.2.2/4.3.3.1/timpani percussion (2) celesta harp/strings
Dedication: Bernard de Nevers [Lengnick]
Duration: 9 minutes
First performance: London, Royal Albert Hall, 5 August 1952.
    BBC Symphony Orchestra, conducted by Malcolm Sargent
Publication: Lengnick, 1951
RECORDING: D24
SEE: B17, B211, B243

OTHER VERSIONS
(1) English Dances (set 2): arranged for piano duet (Reizenstein)
Publication: Lengnick, 1958

W36.   *THE FAIR FIELD* (Opus 110 - 1972)
       Overture for orchestra

       Commissioned by Croydon Arts Festival for the 10th anniversary of the
       opening of the Fairfield Hall
       2+1.2.2.2/4.3.3.1/ timpani percussion (2)/strings
       Dedication: William Walton with the greatest esteem and affection
       Duration: 7½ minutes
       First performance: Croydon, Fairfield Hall, 27 April 1973.
           Royal Philharmonic Orchestra, conducted by Malcolm Arnold
       Publication: Faber Music, 1973 (in conjunction with the CML)
       RECORDING: D26
       SEE: B325, B355

W37.   *FANTASY FOR AUDIENCE AND ORCHESTRA* (Opus 106 - 1970)

       Commissioned by the BBC
       2+1.2.2.2/4.3.3.1/timpani percussion (3) harp organ/strings
       Duration: 13½ minutes
       First performance: London, Royal Albert Hall, 12 September 1970.
           BBC Symphony Orchestra, conducted by Colin Davis
       Unpublished
       SEE: B43, B180, B323, B339, B349

W38.   *FANTASY ON A THEME OF JOHN FIELD FOR PIANO AND
       ORCHESTRA* (Opus 116 - 1975)

       Theme taken from Field's Nocturne in C

2+1.2.2.2/4.3.3.1/timpani percussion (2) harp/strings
Dedication: John Lill
Duration: 20 minutes
First performance: London, Royal Festival Hall, 26 May 1977.
    John Lill (piano) with the Royal Philharmonic Orchestra, conducted
    by Lawrence Foster
Publication: Faber Music, 1975
RECORDING: D32
SEE: B205

W39. *FESTIVAL OVERTURE* (Opus 14 - 1946)

Written for Philip Pfaff
2.2.2.2/2.2.0.0/timpani/strings
Duration: 6 minutes
First performance: Ipswich, Town Hall, c. 1946.
    Ipswich Symphony Orchestra, conducted by Philip Pfaff
Unpublished

W40. *A FLOURISH FOR ORCHESTRA* (Opus 112 - 1973)

Written to celebrate the 500th anniversary of the granting of the charter
of the City of Bristol
2+1..2.2.2/4.3.3.1/timpani percussion (3)/strings
Duration: 4 minutes
First performance: Bristol, Colston Hall, 26 September 1973.
    Bournemouth Symphony Orchestra, conducted by Rudolf Schwarz
Publication: Faber Music, 1973

W41. *FOUR CORNISH DANCES* (Opus 91 - 1966)

I   - Vivace
II - Andantino
III - Con moto e sempre senza parodia
IV - Allegro ma non troppo

2+1.2.2.2/4.3.3.1/timpani percussion (3) harp strings
Dedication: Isobel Arnold
Duration: 10 minutes
First performance: London, Royal Albert Hall, 13 August 1966.
    London Philharmonic Orchestra, conducted by Malcolm Arnold
Publication: Faber Music, 1968
RECORDING: D35

SEE: B70, B299

OTHER VERSIONS
(1) Four Cornish Dances: arranged for concert band (Marciniak)
Publication: Faber Music, 1968
Schirmer (New York), 1975

(2) Four Cornish Dances: arranged for brass band (Farr)
Publication: Faber Music, 1985

W42.   *FOUR IRISH DANCES* (Opus 126 - 1986)

I   - Allegro con energico
II   - Comodo
III   - Piacevole
IV   - Vivace

2+1.2.2.2/4.3.2+1.1/timpani percussion (2) harp/strings
Dedication: Donald Mitchell
Duration: 10 - 11 minutes
First performance: Leeds Castle (Kent), 10 October 1987.
Wren Orchestra, conducted by Malcolm Arnold
Publication: Faber Music, 1986
RECORDING: D36
SEE: B223

W43.   *FOUR SCOTTISH DANCES* (Opus 59 - 1957)

I   - Pesante
II   - Vivace
III   - Allegretto
IV   - Con brio

Commissioned by the BBC for the 1957 BBC Light Music Festival
1+1.2.2.2/4.2.3.0/timpani percussion harp/strings
Duration: 8½ minutes
First performance: London Royal Festival Hall, 8 June 1957.
BBC Concert Orchestra, conducted by Malcolm Arnold
Publication: Paterson, 1957
RECORDING: D37
SEE: B167

OTHER VERSIONS

(1) *Four Scottish Dances:* Arranged for brass band (Farr)
Publication: Paterson, 1984

W44.   *FOUR WELSH DANCES* (Opus 138 - 1989)

I   - Allegro
II   - Poco lento
III - Vivace
IV   - Andante con moto

Commissioned by the Hallé Concerts Society, with funds from Brass
North Ltd.
2+1.2.2.2/4.3.3.1/timpani percussion (2) harp/strings
Dedication: To Emrys Lloyd-Roberts
Duration: c.10 minutes
First performance: Manchester, Free Trade Hall, 19 June 1989.
    Hallé Orchestra, conducted by Owain Arwel Hughes
Publication: Novello, 1989
RECORDING: D38

W45.   *GRAND CONCERTO GASTRONOMIQUE* (Opus 76 - 1961)
For eater, waiter, food and large orchestra. Written for the Hoffnung
Astronautical Music Festival.

1   - Prologue (Maestoso) - Oysters (Moderato - Vivace)
II   - Soup: Brown Windsor (Maestoso - Allegro Vivace)
III - Roast Beef (Nobilmente)
IV   - Cheese (Maestoso)
V   - Peach Melba (Moderato e molto espressivo)
VI   - Coffee, Brandy, Epilogue (Allegro moderato)

2+1.2.2.2/4.3.2.1/timpani percussion (2) harp/strings
Duration: 20 minutes
First performance: London, Royal Festival Hall, 28 November 1961.
    Henry Sherek (eater) with the Morley College Symphony Orchestra,
    conducted by Malcolm Arnold
Unpublished
SEE: B27

W46.   *A GRAND, GRAND OVERTURE* (Opus 57 - 1956)

Written for the 1956 Hoffnung Music Festival
3 vacuum cleaners, 1 floor polisher, 4 rifles -

2+1.2.2.2/4.3.3.1/timpani percussion (2) organ harp/strings
Duration: 8 minutes
First performance: London, Royal Festival Hall, 13 November 1956.
    Morley College Symphony Orchestra with Dennis Brain (organ)
    conducted by Malcolm Arnold
Publication: Paterson, 1956
RECORDING: D39

OTHER VERSIONS
(1) *A Grand, Grand Overture*: arranged for symphonic wind band
(Wilson)
Publication: Paterson and Carl Fischer, 1983

W47.   *LARCH TREES* (Opus 3 - 1943)
Tone poem for orchestra

2.2.2.2/4.0.0.0/strings
Duration: 8½ minutes
First performance: London, Royal Albert Hall, 1 October 1943.
    London Philharmonic Orchestra, conducted by Malcolm Arnold
Publication: Faber, 1985
RECORDING: D45

W48.   *LEONORA [OVERTURE] NO. 4 (BEETHOVEN - STRASSER)* (1961)

Written for the Hoffnung Astronautical Music Festival
2+1.2.2.2/4.2.3.1/timpani percussion (2)/strings, plus 12 trumpets (off
stage) and a street band
Duration: 9½ minutes
First performance: London, Royal Festival Hall, 28 November 1961.
    Morley College Symphony Orchestra, conducted by Norman del
    Mar
Unpublished

W49.   *LITTLE SUITE [NO. 2]* (Opus 78 - 1962)
for orchestra

I   - Overture (Allegro moderato)
II   - Ballad (Andantino)
III   - Dance (Vivace)

Written for the Farnham Festival
2.2.2.2/4.3.2.1/timpani percussion (3)/strings

Duration: 10 minutes
First performance: Farnham, Parish Church, 13 May 1963.
    Combined orchestra of Farnham Grammar School and Tiffin
    School, conducted by Dennis Bloodworth
First London: Royal Festival Hall, 15 May 1964.
    London Junior and Senior Orchestras, conducted by Oliver Broome
Publication: Paterson, 1963
RECORDING: D49
SEE: B168, B278, B368

W50.   *A MANX SUITE - THIRD LITTLE SUITE* (Opus 142 - 1990)

    I   - Allegretto
    II   - Allegro
    III - Allegretto
    IV   - Lento
    V   - Allegretto

Commissioned by: Alan Pickard, Music Advisor, Isle of Man
        Department of Education for the Manx Youth Orchestra under the
        patronage of the Isle of Man Bank Ltd in celebration of the Bank's
        125th anniversary
2+1.2.2.2+1/4.3.2+1.1/timpani percussion (2) harp/strings
Duration: 10 minutes
First performance: Douglas (IoM), Villa Marina, 8 December 1990.
        Manx Youth Orchestra, conducted by Malcolm Arnold
First London: unable to trace
Publication: Novello, 1990
RECORDING: D50

W51.   *PETERLOO* (Opus 97 - 1968)
        Overture for orchestra

Commissioned by the Trades Union Congress for the 100th anniversary
of its first meeting in 1868
2+1.2.2.2/4.3.3.1/timpani percussion (4) harp/strings
Duration: c. 10 minutes
First performance: London, Royal Festival Hall, 7 June 1968.
        Royal Philharmonic Orchestra, conducted by Malcolm Arnold
Publication: Faber Music, 1979
RECORDING: D53
SEE: B340

W52.   *PHILHARMONIC CONCERTO* (Opus 120 - 1976)
for orchestra

I   - Intrada (Vivace)
II   - Aria (Andantino)
III   - Chacony (Energico)

Commissioned by the Commercial Union Insurance Company for the
London Philharmonic Orchestra's bicentennial tour of the USA in 1976
2+1.2+1.2.2+1/4.3.3.1/timpani percussion (3) harp strings
Duration: 13 minutes
First performance: London, Royal Festival Hall, 31 October 1976.
     London Philharmonic Orchestra, conducted by Bernard Haitink
First USA: Chicago, Symphony Hall, 7 November 1976.
     London Philharmonic Orchestra, conducted by Bernard Haitink
Publication: Faber Music, 1976
SEE: B41

W53.   *POPULAR BIRTHDAY* (1972)
for orchestra

One of six pieces written to celebrate the 70th birthday of Sir William
Walton on 29 March 1972
1+2.2.2.2/4.3.2.1/timpani percussion (2) harp/strings
Dedication: For the 70th birthday of Sir William Walton, O.M., with
homage and every expression of friendship
Duration: 1 minute
First performance: London, Royal Festival Hall, 28 March 1972.
     London Symphony Orchestra, conducted by Malcolm Arnold
Unpublished
RECORDING: D54

OTHER VERSIONS
(1) *Popular Birthday:* reduced version
Unpublished

W54.   *ROBERT KETT OVERTURE* Opus 141 - 1990)

Commissioned by the Education Department of the Norfolk County
Council
2+1.2.2.2/4.3.2+1.1/timpani percussion (4)/strings
Duration: 8 minutes
First performance: Norwich, St Andrew's Hall, 25 July 1990.

Norfolk Youth Orchestra, conducted by Simon Halsey
First London: unable to trace
Publication: Novello, 1990

W55.   *A SALUTE TO THOMAS MERRITT* (Opus 98 - 1967)
for two brass bands and orchestra

Written to celebrate the 60th anniversary of the death of the Cornish
composer Thomas Merritt
2+1.2.2.2/4.3.3.1/timpani percussion (4) harp/strings
Duration: 5 minutes
First performance: Truro, the Cathedral, 16 March 1968.
St. Dennis Silver Band, St. Agnes Silver Band, Penzance
Orchestral Society, Cornwall Symphony Orchestra, conducted by
Malcolm Arnold
Unpublished

W56.   *SERENADE FOR THE GUITAR AND STRINGS* (Opus 50 - 1955)

Dedication: Julian Bream [for whom it was written]
Duration: 5½ minutes
First performance: Richmond (Surrey), Community Centre Hall,
Summer 1955.
Julian Bream (guitar) with the Richmond Community Centre String
Orchestra, conducted by Malcolm Arnold
First London: Wigmore Hall, 11 June 1956.
Julian Bream (guitar) with the Kalmar Chamber Orchestra,
conducted by Leonard Friedman
Publication: Paterson, 1955

W57.   *SERENADE FOR SMALL ORCHESTRA* (Opus 26 - 1950)

I   - Allegretto
II   - Andante con moto
III   - Allegro vivace

2.2.2.2/2.2.0.0/timpani/strings
Duration: 13½ minutes
First performance: London, Hampton Court, The Orangery, 4 June
1950. New London Orchestra, conducted by Alec Sherman
Publication: Lengnick, 1950
RECORDING: D59

W58.   *SHAKESPEAREAN CELLO CONCERTO* (Opus 136 - 1988)
       for cello and orchestra

       I   - Allegro
       II   - Lento
       III   - Vivace

       Commissioned by the Royal Philharmonic Society with additional funds
       provided by Greater London Arts
       2+1.2.2.2/4.3.3.1/timpani percussion (1)/strings
       Dedication: To Julian Lloyd Webber
       Duration: 25 minutes
       First performance: London, Royal Festival Hall, 9 March 1989.
             Julian Lloyd Webber (cello) with the Royal Philharmonic
             Orchestra, conducted by Vernon Handley
       Publication: Novello, 1989
       SEE: B34, B217

W59.   *SINFONIETTA [NO. 1]* (Opus 48 - 1954)
       for orchestra

       I   - Allegro commodo
       II   - Allegretto
       III   - Allegro con brio

       0.2.0.0/2.0.0.0/strings
       Dedication: Boyd Neel Orchestra
       Duration: 12 minutes
       First performance: Nottingham, Albert Hall, 3 December 1954.
             Boyd Neel Orchestra, conducted by Anthony Collins
       First London: Royal Festival Hall, 7 March 1955.
             Boyd Neel Orchestra, conducted by Anthony Collins
       Publication: Paterson, 1955
       RECORDING: D61
       SEE: B65, B277, B290

W60.   *SINFONIETTA [NO. 2]* (Opus 65 - 1958)
       for orchestra

       I   - Allegro non troppo
       II   - Lento
       III   - Allegro con brio

Written for the 21st anniversary of the Jacques Orchestra
2.0.0.0/2.0.0.0/strings
Dedication: "For J" [Reginald Jacques]
Duration: 12½ minutes
First performance: London, Victoria and Albert Museum, 15 June
     1958. Jacques Orchestra, conducted by Reginald Jacques
Publication: Paterson, 1958
RECORDING: D62

W61.   *SINFONIETTA [NO. 3]* (Opus 81 - 1964)
       for orchestra

        I   - Allegro vivace
        II   - Vivace
        III   - Andante con moto
        IV   - Allegro con energico

       1.2.0.2/2.0.0.0/strings
       Duration: 14½ minutes
       First performance: Croydon, Fairfield Hall, 30 January 1965.
            New Philharmonia Orchestra, conducted by Malcolm Arnold
       Publication: Paterson, 1964
       SEE: B8

W62.   *THE SMOKE* (Opus 21 - 1948)
       Overture for orchestra

       2+1.2.2.2/4.3.3.1/timpani percussion (3) harp/strings
       Dedication: Rudolf Schwarz and the Bournemouth Municipal Orchestra
       Duration: 7 minutes
       First performance: London, Royal Albert Hall, 24 October 1948.
            Bournemouth Municipal Orchestra, conducted by Rudolf Schwarz
       Publication: Lengnick, 1948
       RECORDING: D63
       SEE: B229

W63.   *A SUNSHINE OVERTURE* (Opus 83 - 1964)
       For orchestra

       Written for the Sunshine Home for Blind Babies
       2.2.2.2/2.2.1.0/percussion/strings
       Duration: 2 minutes
       First performance: London, Palace Theatre, 14 July 1964.

Sunshine Gala Orchestra, conducted by Dudley Simpson
Unpublished

W64. *A SUSSEX OVERTURE* (Opus 31 - 1951)
For orchestra

Commissioned for the 1951 Festival of Brighton
2+1.2.2.2/4.3.3.1/timpani percussion (2)/ strings
Dedication: Herbert Menges and the Brighton Philharmonic Society
Duration: 8½ minutes
First performance: Brighton, The Dome, 29 July 1951.
    Southern Philharmonic Orchestra, conducted by Herbert Menges
Publication: Lengnick, 1951
RECORDING: D68

W65. *SYMPHONIC SUITE FOR ORCHESTRA* (Opus 12 - 1945)

I   - Allegro giubiloso
II   - Elegy (Andante con moto)
III - Andante moderato e molto sostenuto

3.2.2.2/4.3.3.1/timpani percussion (2)/strings
Dedication: Written in memory of the composer's brother Philip, killed
                in World War II
Duration: 15 minutes
First performance: unable to trace
Unpublished

W66. *SYMPHONY FOR STRINGS* (Opus 13 - 1946)

I   - Allegro ma non troppo
II   - Andante quasi allegretto
III - Allegro feroce

Written for the Riddick String Orchestra
Duration: 24 minutes
First performance: London, Kensington Town Hall, 29 April 1947.
    Riddick String Orchestra, conducted by Kathleen Riddick
Publication: Lengnick, 1947

W67. *SYMPHONY NO. 1* (Opus 22 - 1949)
for orchestra

I   - Allegro
II   - Andantino
II   - Vivace con fuoco - Alla marcia - Maestoso

3.2.2.2/4.3.3.1/timpani percussion harp/strings
Duration: 28½ minutes
First performance: Cheltenham, Town Hall, 6 July 1951.
     Hallé Orchestra, conducted by Malcolm Arnold
First London: Royal Festival Hall, 16 November 1951.
     London Philharmonic Orchestra, conducted by Malcolm Arnold
Publication: Lengnick, 1952
RECORDING: D70
SEE: B25, B57, B171, B208. B226, B369

W68.   *SYMPHONY NO. 2* (Opus 40 - 1953)
       for orchestra

I   - Allegretto
II   - Vivace
III - Lento
IV   - Allegro con brio - Lento molto e maestoso

  Commissioned by the Winter Gardens Society, Bournemouth
2+1.2.2.2+1/4.3.3.1/timpani percussion harp/strings
Dedication: Charles Groves and the Bournemouth Municipal Orchestra,
                in celebration of their Diamond Jubilee
Duration: 30 minutes
First performance: Bournemouth, Winter Gardens, 25 May 1953.
     Bournemouth Municipal Orchestra, conducted by Charles Groves
First London: Royal Festival Hall, 3 June 1954.
     London Philharmonic Orchestra, conducted by Malcolm Arnold
Publication: Paterson, 1953
RECORDING: D71
SEE: B18, B58, B59, B67, B104, B181, B234, B237, B289, B363

W69.   *SYMPHONY NO. 3* (Opus 63 - 1957)
       for orchestra

I   - Allegro - Vivace
II   - Lento
III - Allegro con brio - Presto - Lento e maestoso - Presto

Commissioned by the Royal Liverpool Philharmonic Society

2+1.2.2.2/4.3.3.1/timpani/strings
Dedication: The Royal Liverpool Philharmonic Society
Duration: 32½ minutes
First performance: London. Royal Festival Hall, 2 December 1957
      Royal Liverpool Philharmonic Orchestra, conducted by John
      Pritchard
Publication: Paterson, 1958
RECORDING: D72
SEE: B37, B72, B174, B236, B275

W70.   *SYMPHONY NO. 4* (Opus 71 - 1960)
        for orchestra

        I   - Allegro
        II   - Vivace ma non troppo
        III - Andantino
        IV   - Con fuoco - Alla marcia - Tempo primo - Maestoso - Allegro
        molto

        Commissioned by the BBC
        2+1.2.2.2+1/4.3.3.1/timpani percussion (3) celesta harp/strings
        Duration: 36 minutes
        First performance: London, Royal Festival Hall, 2 November 1960.
            BBC Symphony Orchestra, conducted by Malcolm Arnold
        Publication: Paterson, 1960
        RECORDING: D73
        SEE: B20, B75, B113, B173, B293, B346, B347

W71.   *SYMPHONY NO. 5* (Opus 74 - 1961)
        for orchestra

        I   - Tempestuoso
        II   - Andante con moto - Adagio
        III - Con fuoco
        IV   - Risoluto - Lento

        Commissioned by the Cheltenham Festival Society
        2+1.2.2.2/4.3.3.1/timpani percussion (2) celesta harp/strings
        Duration: 33 minutes
        First performance: Cheltenham, Town Hall, 3 July 1961.
            Hallé Orchestra, conducted by Malcolm Arnold
        First London: Royal Festival Hall, 16 December 1971.
            New Philharmonic Orchestra, conducted by Malcolm Arnold

Publication: Paterson, 1960
RECORDING: D74
SEE: B28, B224, B294, B350, B371

W72.   *SYMPHONY NO. 6* (Opus 95 - 1967)
for orchestra

I   - Energico
II   - Lento
III   - Con fuoco

2+1.2.2.2/4.3.3.1/timpani percussion (3)/strings
Duration: 26 minutes
First performance: Sheffield, City Hall, 28 June 1968.
    BBC Northern Symphony Orchestra, conducted by Malcolm Arnold
First London: Royal Albert Hall, 24 September 1969.
    Royal Philharmonic Orchestra, conducted by Malcolm Arnold
Publication: Faber Music, 1974
RECORDING: D75
SEE: B151. B152, B255

W73.   *SYMPHONY NO. 7* (Opus 113 - 1973)
for orchestra

I   - Allegro energico [Katherine]
II   - Andante con moto - Molto vivace - Lento [Robert]
III   - Allegro - Allegretto - Allegro - Allegretto - Allegro [Edward]

Commissioned by the New Philharmonia Orchestra
2+1.2.2.2+1/4.3.3.1/timpani percussion (3) harp/strings
Dedication: The composer's children, Katherine, Robert and Edward
Duration: 45 minutes
First performance: London, Royal Festival Hall, 5 May 1974.
    New Philharmonic Orchestra, conducted by Malcolm Arnold
Publication: Faber Music, 1974
RECORDING: D76
SEE: B149, B351

W74.   *SYMPHONY NO. 8* (Opus 124 - 1978)
for orchestra

I   - Allegro
II   - Andantino

III   - Vivace

Commissioned by the Rustam K. Kermani Foundation in memory of Rustam K. Kermani
2+1.2.2.2/4.3.3.1/timpani percussion (2) harp/strings
Duration: 25 minutes
First performance: Albany, New York (USA), Troy Savings Bank Music Hall, 5 May 1979.
 Albany Symphony Orchestra, conducted by Julius Hegyi
First British: Manchester, Royal Northern College of Music, 2 October 1981.
 BBC Northern Symphony Orchestra, conducted by Charles Groves
First London: St John's, Smith Square, 26 November 1982.
 Young Musicians' Symphony Orchestra, conducted by James Blair
Publication: Faber Music, 1981
 (Published, mistakenly, as Opus 121)
RECORDING: D77
SEE: B9, B45, B240

W75. *SYMPHONY NO. 9* (Opus 128 - 1986)
 for orchestra

  I   - Vivace
  II   - Allegretto
  III - Giubiloso
  IV   - Lento

2+1.2.2.2/4.3.3.1/timpani percussion (2) harp/strings
Dedication: Anthony John Day
Duration: 52 minutes
First performance: Manchester, BBC Studio 7, 20 January 1992.
 BBC Philharmonic Orchestra, conducted by Charles Groves
First London: Royal Festival Hall, 19 October 1996.
 London Festival Orchestra, conducted by Ross Popple
Unpublished
RECORDING: D78
SEE: B42, B115

W76. *TAM O'SHANTER* (Opus 51 - 1955)
 Overture for orchestra

2+1.2.2.2/4.3.3.1/timpani percussion (2)/strings
Dedication: Michael Diack [Paterson]

Duration: 7½ minutes
First performance: London, Royal Albert Hall, 16 August 1955.
   Royal Philharmonic Orchestra, conducted by Malcolm Arnold
Publication: Paterson, 1955
RECORDING: D79
SEE: B12, B63, B76, B77, B78, B161, B238, B283, B319

W77.   *THEME AND VARIATION* (1966)
for orchestra. Contribution to the Severn Bridge Variations written to
mark the opening of the Severn Bridge and the first visit to Wales of the
BBC Training Orchestra on its first birthday. Other contributions were
written by Alun Hoddinott, Nicholas Maw, Daniel Jones, Grace
Williams and Michael Tippett.

Commissioned by the BBC
3.2+1.2+1.0/4.3.3.1/timpani percussion (2) harp/strings
Duration: 19 minutes (whole work)
First performance: Swansea, Brangwyn Hall, 11 January 1967.
   BBC Training Orchestra, conducted by Adrian Boult
First London: Royal Albert Hall, 20 July 1976.
   BBC Welsh Symphony Orchestra, conducted by Boris Brott
Unpublished
SEE: B251

W78.   *TO YOUTH* (1948)
Suite for orchestra

   I   - Prelude (Maestoso)
   II   - Pastoral (Allegretto)
   III   - March (Allegro con brio)

Written for the National Youth Orchestra of Great Britain
2.2.2.2/4.3.2.1/timpani percussion (2)/strings
Duration: 9½ minutes
First performance: Bath, The Pavilion, 21 April 1948.
   National Youth Orchestra of Great Britain, conducted by Reginald
   Jacques

OTHER VERSIONS
(1) In 1955, Arnold renamed "To Youth" Little Suite No. 1 (for
   orchestra) which became Opus 53, with the central movement
   retitled Dance (Allegretto)
Publication: Paterson, 1956

SEE: B69

(2) <u>March</u>: arranged for Military Band (Sumner)
Publication: Paterson, 1965
RECORDING: D48

W79. *TOY SYMPHONY* (Opus 62 - 1957)

I   - Allegro
II   - Allegretto
III - Vivace

12 toy instruments: quail cuckoo whistle, 3 trumpets, 3 dulcimers,
triangle, cymbal, drum/piano/string quartet
Dedication: The Musicians' Benevolent Fund
Duration: 9½ minutes
First performance: London, Savoy Hotel, 28 November 1957.
    Denis Truscott, Thomas Armstrong, Edric Cundell, W. Greenhouse
    Alt, Gerard Hoffnung, Eileen Joyce, Steuart Wilson, George Baker,
    David McBain, Leslie Woodgate, Eric Coates, Astra Desmond with
    the Amici String Quartet and Joseph Cooper (piano), conducted by
    Malcolm Arnold
Publication: Paterson, 1958
SEE: B160

W80. *UNITED NATIONS* (1958)
for four military bands, organ and orchestra

Commissioned for the 1958 Hoffnung Interplanetary Music Festival
2+1.2.2.2/4.3.3.1/timpani percussion (3)/strings
Duration: 13 minutes
First performance: London, Royal Festival Hall, 21 November 1958.
    Band of the RMSM, Kneller Hall and Morley College Symphony
    Orchestra, conducted by Malcolm Arnold
Unpublished

W81. *VARIATIONS FOR ORCHESTRA ON A THEME OF RUTH GIPPS*
(Opus 122 - 1977)
Theme (taken from Ruth Gipps's 1953 <u>Coronation March</u>) (Allegro
moderato)

I   - Vivace
II   - Alla marcia

III - Lento
IV - Vivace
V   - Allegretto
VI - Finale (Maestoso)

1+1.2.2.2/2.2.0.0/timpani/strings
Duration: 13 minutes
First performance: London, Queen Elizabeth Hall, 22 February 1978.
  Chanticleer Orchestra, conducted by Ruth Gipps
Publication: Faber Music, 1978
Recording: D87

IV.   CHAMBER AND SOLO INSTRUMENTAL MUSIC

W82.   *ALLEGRO IN E MINOR FOR PIANO* (1937)

Duration: 35 seconds
First performance: unable to trace
Unpublished
RECORDING: D1

W83.   *CHILDREN'S SUITE FOR PIANO* (Opus 16 - 1947)

I   - Prelude (Allegretto)
II   - Carol (Andante con moto)
III - Shepherd's Lament (Andante con molto espressivo)
IV   - Trumpet Tune (Allegro)
V   - Blue Tune (Andante moderato)
VI   - Folk Song (Allegro vivace)

Duration: 4 minutes
First performance: unable to trace
Unpublished
RECORDING: D5

W84.   *CONCERT PIECE FOR PERCUSSION* (1958)
for 3 percussion players and piano

Written for BBC Television
Piano/3 timpani/side drum, bass drum, cymbal, tambourine, tam-tam,
wood block, triangle, xylophone, glockenspiel, whip, maracas, bongo

Dedication: James Blades
Duration: 4½ minutes
First performance: unable to trace
Publication: Faber Music, 1984

OTHER VERSIONS
(1) Arrangement for 1 percussion player and piano (Blades)
Publication: Faber Music, 1984

W85.   *DAY DREAMS* (1938)
for solo piano

Duration: 3½ minutes
First performance: unable to trace
Unpublished
RECORDING: D20

W86.   *DIVERTIMENTO FOR WIND TRIO* (Opus 37 - 1952)
for flute, oboe and clarinet

I   - Allegro energico
II   - Languido
III   - Vivace
IV   - Andantino - Lento
V   - Maestoso - Prestissimo
VI   - Piacevole

Duration: 8¾ minutes
First performance: London, Mercury Theatre (Notting Hill Gate), c.1953.
        Richard Adeney (flute), Sidney Sutcliffe (oboe) and Stephen Waters
        (clarinet)
Publication: Paterson, 1952
RECORDING: 21
SEE: B56, B61

W87.   *DUO FOR FLUTE AND VIOLA* (Opus 10 - 1945)

I   - Andante quasi allegretto
II   - Allegro
III   - Allegretto ma non troppo

Duration: 13 minutes
First performance: London, Salle Erard, 3 December 1946.

John Francis (flute) and Bernard Davies (viola)
Publication: Faber Music, 1985

W88.   *DUO FOR TWO Bb CLARINETS* (Opus 135 - 1988)

I   - Allegro energico
II   - Allegretto
III - Vivace
IV - Lento
V   - Vivace
VI - Adagio

Duration: unable to trace
First performance: unable to trace
Unpublished

W89.   *DUO FOR TWO CELLOS* (Opus 85 - 1965)

Duration: 5 minutes
Publication: Novello, 1971 (in Hugo Cole and Anne Shuttleworth:
              Playing the Cello)

OTHER VERSIONS
(1) Arrangement for two violas (Milne)
Publication: Novello, 1986 (Playing the Viola)

W90.   *EIGHT CHILDREN'S PIECES FOR PIANO* (Opus 36 - 1952)

I   - Tired Bagpipes (Slow)
II   - Two Sad Hands (Slow)
III - Across the Plains (Slow)
IV - Strolling Tune (Andantino)
V   - Dancing Tune (Allegro)
VI - Giants (Pesante e poco lento)
VII - The Duke Goes A-Hunting (Vivace)
VIII - The Buccaneer (Vivace e con brio)

Duration: 9½ minutes
First performance: unable to trace
Publication: Lengnick, 1952
RECORDING: D22

OTHER VERSIONS

(1)   *CHILDRENS SUITE* (1995)
8 piano pieces (Opus 36) orchestrated by D. Bloodworth
2.2.2.2/4.3.3.1/timpani percussion/strings
Unpublished

W91.   *FANTASY FOR BASSOON* (Opus 86 - 1965)

Commissioned by the City of Birmingham Symphony Orchestra for the
Birmingham International Wind Competition in May 1966
Duration: 4½ minutes
First performance: Birmingham, Town Hall, May 1966.
        František Herman (bassoon)
Publication: Faber Music, 1966
SEE: B210

W92.   *FANTASY FOR CELLO* (Opus 130 - 1987)

Commissioned by Julian Lloyd Webber
Dedication: For Julian Lloyd Webber
Duration: c.16 minutes
First performance: London Wigmore Hall, 13 December 1987.
        Julian Lloyd Webber (cello)
Publication: Faber Music, 1988 (edited by Julian Lloyd Webber)
RECORDING: D28
SEE: B39

W93.   *FANTASY FOR CLARINET* (OPUS 87 - 1965)

Commissioned by the City of Birmingham Symphony Orchestra for the
Birmingham International Wind Competition in May 1966
Duration: 4½ minutes
First performance: Birmingham, Town Hall, May 1966.
        Aurelian - Octav Popa (clarinet)
Publication: Faber Music, 1966
RECORDING: D29

W94.   *FANTASY FOR FLUTE* (Opus 89 - 1965)

Commissioned by the City of Birmingham Symphony Orchestra for the
Birmingham International Wind Competition in May 1966
Duration: 4½ minutes
First performance: Birmingham, Town Hall, May 1966.
        James Galway (flute)

Publication: Faber Music, 1966

W95.   *FANTASY FOR GUITAR* (Opus 107 - 1970)

      I   - Prelude (Maestoso)
      II   - Scherzo (Allegro)
      III   - Arietta (Andante con moto)
      IV   - Fughetta - Arietta (Semplice e languido)
      V   - March (Allegro)
      VI   - Postlude (Maestoso)

Dedication: Julian Bream
Duration: 10 minutes
First performance: London, Queen Elizabeth Hall, 16 May 1971.
      Julian Bream (guitar)
Publication: Faber Music, 1971

W96.   *FANTASY FOR HARP* (Opus 117 - 1975)

      I   - Lament (Maestoso)
      II   - March - Nocturne (Andante con moto)
      III   - Scherzo (Vivace)
      IV   - Finale (Maestoso)

Dedication: Osian Ellis
Duration: 11 minutes
First performance: London, Law Society Hall, 27 January 1976.
      Osian Ellis (harp)
Publication: Faber Music, 1976 (edited by Osian Ellis)
Recording: D30

W97.   *FANTASY FOR HORN* (Opus 88 - 1965)

Commissioned for the City of Birmingham Symphony Orchestra for the
Birmingham International Wind Competition in May 1966
Duration: 4½ minutes
First performance: Birmingham, Town Hall, May 1966.
      Farenc Tarjáni (horn)
Publication: Faber Music, 1966

W98.   *FANTASY FOR OBOE* (Opus 90 - 1965)

Commissioned for the City of Birmingham Symphony Orchestra for the

Birmingham International Wind Competition in May 1966
Duration: 4½ minutes
First performance: Birmingham, Town Hall, May 1966.
       Maurice Bourgue (oboe)
Publication: Faber Music, 1966
RECORDING: D31

W99.   *FANTASY FOR RECORDER* (Opus 127 - 1986)

Commissioned by Wingfield Arts and Music
Dedication: Michala Petri
Duration: 11 minutes
First performance: Beccles, Parish Church of St Michael, 11 July 1987.
       Michala Petri (recorder)
Publication: Faber Music, 1986

W100.   *FANTASY FOR RECORDER AND STRING QUARTET* (Opus 140 - 1990)

Theme and variations in five movements:
I   - Andante e Mesto
II   - Allegro
III   - Lento e Mesto
IV   - Allegretto
V   - Vivace

Commissioned for Michala Petri by the Carnegie Hall Corporation in honour of the Carnegie Hall's Centennial Season
Dedication: Michala Petri
Duration: 20 minutes
First performance: New York, Carnegie Hall, Weill Recital Hall, 15
       March 1991. Michala Petri (recorder) and the Cavani String
       Quartet
First British: Manchester, University Music Department, 15 November
       1991. Evelyn Nallen (recorder) and the Lindsay String Quartet
Publication: Novello, 1991
SEE: B22, B297

OTHER VERSIONS
(1) Fantasy: arranged for string orchestra (Easterbrook)

First performance: Harrogate, Royal Hall, 6 August 1991.
       Michala Petri (recorder) and the Guildhall String Ensemble,

conducted by Robert Salter
Unpublished

W101.   *FANTASY FOR TROMBONE* (Opus 101 - 1969)

Duration: 4 minutes
First performance: unable to trace
Publication: Faber Music, 1969

W102.   *FANTASY FOR TRUMPET* (Opus 100 - 1969)

Dedication: Ernest Hall
Duration: 4 minutes
First performance: unable to trace
Publication: Faber Music, 1969
SEE: B93

W103.   *FANTASY FOR TUBA* (Opus 102 - 1969)

Duration: 4 minutes
First performance: unable to trace
Publication: Faber Music, 1969

W104.   *FIVE PIECES FOR VIOLIN AND PIANO* (Opus 84 - 1964)

I   - Prelude (Con energico)
II   - Aubade (Vivace)
III   - Waltz (Grazioso)
IV   - Ballad (Andantino)
V   - Moto Perpetuo (Presto): dedicated to Charlie Parker

Written for Yehudi Menuhin to use as encore pieces on a USA tour
Duration: 9 minutes
First performance: Northumberland, Bamburgh Castle, 24 July 1965.
        Yehudi Menuhin (violin) and Ivor Newton (piano)
Publication: Paterson , 1965
RECORDING: D34

W105.   *FOUR PIECES FOR CHAMBER ENSEMBLE* (1959)
for recorder and 3 violins

I   - Prelude (Allegro moderato)
II   - Waltz (Allegro)

III   - Chorale (Andante)
IV   - Carillon (Allegro moderato)

Written as practice material for the Arnold family
Duration: 4 minutes
First performance: unable to trace
Unpublished

W106. *GRAND FANTASIA* ("Opus 973" - [c.1938])
      For flute, trumpet and piano [composed by A. Youngman]
      Adapted from the figured bass by Basil C. Youngman
      Andante Espressivo; Czhrdas; Presto; Tango; Blues; Waltz; Andante
      Espressivo
      First performance: unable to trace
      Unpublished

W107. *HAILE SELASSIE* (1936)
      March for solo piano

      Duration: unable to trace
      First performance: unable to trace
      Unpublished

W108. *KATHERINE, WALKING AND RUNNING* (1953)
      for two violins

      Written for his daughter Katherine to play with a school friend
      Duration: 40 seconds
      First performance: unable to trace
      Unpublished

W109. *OVERTURE FOR WIND OCTET* (1940)
      Arranged for piano duet

      First performance: unable to trace
      Unpublished

      OTHER VERSIONS
      (1) *Overture* - arranged for string orchestra by P. Wood (1993)
      Unpublished

W110. *PHANTASY FOR STRING QUARTET* (1941)
      Originally entitled "Vita Abundans" this work was placed second in the

W.W. Cobbett prize for composition in 1941

Duration: 12 minutes
First performance: unable to trace
Unpublished

W111.   *PRELUDE FOR PIANO* (1945)

Duration: c. 3 minutes
First performance: unable to trace
Unpublished
RECORDING: D55

W112.   *QUARTET FOR OBOE AND STRINGS* (Opus 61 - 1957)
Written for Leon Goossens on the occasion of his 60th birthday

I   - Allegro non troppo
II   - Allegretto
III   - Vivace con brio

Dedication: Leon Goossens
Duration: 12¾ minutes
First performance: Cambridge, University Music School, 2 May 1957.
    Leon Goossens (oboe) and the Carter String Trio
Publication: Faber Music, 1966

W113.   *QUARTET FOR STRINGS [NO. 1]* (Opus 23 - 1949)

I   - Allegro commodo
II   - Vivace
III   - Andante- Lento - Tempo primo
IV   - Allegro con spirito

Duration: 18¾ minutes
First concert performance: London, I.C.A., 26 October 1951.
    New London String Quartet
Publication: Lengnick, 1951
RECORDING: D56
SEE: B25, B54, B116, B228, B242, B288

W114.   *QUARTET FOR STRINGS [NO. 2]* (Opus 118 - 1975)

I   - Allegro

II   - Maestoso con molto rubato - Allegro vivace
III   - Andante
IV   - Allegretto - Vivace - Lento

Dedication: Hugh Maguire
Duration: 29 minutes
First performance: Dublin, the Castle, 9 June 1976.
     Allegri String Quartet
First British: Snape, The Maltings, 12 June 1976.
     Allegri String Quartet
Publication: Faber Music, 1976
RECORDING: D57
SEE: B116, B248

W115. *QUINTET FOR FLUTE, VIOLIN, VIOLA, HORN AND BASSOON*
       (Opus 7 - 1944)

       I   - Allegro con brio
       II   - Andante con moto
       III - Allegretto con molto espressivo

Duration: unable to trace
First performance: London, National Gallery, 21 December 1944.
     Richard Adeney (flute), Albert Chasey (violin), Wrayburn
     Glasspool (viola), Charles Gregory (horn) and George Alexandra
     (bassoon)

REVISED VERSION (1960)
Duration: 13½ minutes
First performance: London, Maida Vale Studios (BBC), 8 March 1960.
     Geoffrey Gilbert (flute), Granville Jones (violin), Frederick Riddle
     (violin), Alan Civil (horn) and Gwydion Brooke (bassoon)
Publication: Paterson, 1960

W116. *QUINTET FOR WIND* (Opus 2 - 1942)

       I   - Allegro
       II   - Presto
       III - Alla marcia

Duration: 13 minutes
First performance: London Trinity College of Music, 7 June 1943.
     London Philharmonic Orchestra Wind Quintet

Unpublished
SEE: B119

W117. *SERENADE IN G FOR PIANO* (1937)

Duration: 2¼ minutes
First performance: unable to trace
Unpublished
RECORDING: D60

W118. *SONATA FOR FLUTE AND PIANO* (1942)

I   - Andante con moto - Allegro
II   - Recitative - Allegro
III   - Allegro

Duration: 8½ minutes
First performance: unable to trace
Unpublished

W119. *SONATA FOR FLUTE AND PIANO* (Opus 121 - 1977)

I   - Allegro
II   - Andante
III   - Maestoso con molto ritmico - Lento molto - A tempo - Lento
        molto - A tempo - Prestissimo

Commissioned by the Welsh Arts Council
Dedication: James Galway
Duration: 14 minutes
First performance: Cardiff, New Hall, 19 March 1977.
        James Galway (flute) and David Johns (piano)
Publication: Faber Music, 1980
SEE: B108

W120. *SONATA FOR PIANO IN B MINOR* (1942)

I   - Allegro ma non troppo
II   - Andante con moto
III   - Alla marcia

Duration: c. 10 minutes
First performance: London, British Music Information Centre, 15 May

1984.
Richard Deering (piano)
Publication: Robertson, 1984
RECORDING: D64

OTHER VERSIONS
(1) *Saxophone Concerto* (1994)
An arrangement of the Piano Sonata for alto saxophone and strings by
David Ellis (1994), made at the request of the composer
First performance: Milton Keynes, Stantonbury Campus Theatre, 10
February 1996.
Gerard McChrystal (saxophone) with the Milton Keynes City Orchestra,
conducted by Hilary Davan Wetton
Unpublished

W121.   *SONATA FOR VIOLA AND PIANO* (Opus 17 - 1947)

   I   - Andante - Adagio - Tempo primo
   II   - Allegretto grazioso - Andante - Tempo primo
   III   - Presto feroce - Adagio - Alla marcia - Andante - Presto feroce -
          Adagio - Prestissimo

Dedication: Frederick Riddle
Duration: 13 minutes
First performance: BBC Latin American Service, 1948.
       F. Riddle (violin) with unknown pianist
First broadcast: BBC Third Programme, 22 November 1949.
       Watson Forbes (viola) and Alan Richardson (piano)
Publication: Lengnick, 1948

W122.   *SONATA [NO. 1] FOR VIOLIN AND PIANO* (Opus 15 - 1947)

   I   - Allegretto
   II   - Andante tranquillo - Allegro iracondamente - Tempo primo
   III   - Allegro vivace-Presto

Duration: 15 minutes
First performance: London , Arts Council, 2 October 1951.
       Nona Liddell (violin) and Daphne Ibbott (piano)
Publication: Lengnick, 1947

W123.   *SONATA [NO. 2] FOR VIOLIN AND PIANO* (Opus 43 - 1953)

Duration: 9 minutes
First performance: London, Royal Festival Hall, 21 October 1953.
        Suzanne Rozsa (viola) and Paul Hamburger (piano)
Publication: Paterson, 1953
SEE: B234, B287

W124.   *SONATINA FOR CLARINET AND PIANO* (Opus 29 - 1951)

        I   - Allegro con brio
        II   - Andantino
        III   - Furioso

Duration: 7¾ minutes
First performance: London, Royal Society of British Artists, 20 March
        1951. Colin Davis (clarinet) and Geoffrey Corbett (piano)
Publication: Lengnick, 1951
RECORDING: D65
SEE: B209, B276, B332

W125.   *SONATINA FOR FLUTE AND PIANO* (Opus 19 - 1948)

        I   - Allegro
        II   - Andante
        III   - Allegretto languido

Dedication: Richard Adeney
Duration: 8 minutes
First broadcast performance: BBC Third Programme, 20 October 1952.
        Richard Adeney (flute) and Frederick Stone (piano)
Publication: Lengnick, 1948
SEE: B241

OTHER VERSIONS
(1)   *Blues* (from the Sonatina), arranged for flute and string orchestra
        by Christopher Palmer
Unpublished

W126.   *SONATINA FOR OBOE AND PIANO* (Opus 28 - 1951)

        I   - Leggiero
        II   - Andante con moto
        III   - Vivace

Duration: 7½ minutes
First performance: Manchester, (Royal) Northern College of Music, 15
January 1952.
        Leon Goossens (oboe) and John Wilson (piano)
Publication: Lengnick, 1951
SEE: B53, B332

OTHER VERSIONS
(1)   Concertino for Oboe and Strings (Opus 28a)
        - orchestratred by Roger Steptoe
RECORDING: D7

W127.   *SONATINA FOR RECORDER AND PIANO* (Opus 41 - 1953)
        (Or flute and piano/oboe and piano).

        I   - Cantilena (Piacevole)
        II   - Chaconne (Andante con moto)
        III   - Rondo (Allegro vivace - Poco meno mosso - Tempo primo -
                 Presto)

Dedication: Philip Rodgers [for whom it was written]
Duration: 7¾ minutes
First broadcast performance: Manchester, BBC Home Service, 14 July
1953. Philip Rodgers (recorder) and Albert Hardie (piano).
Publication: Paterson, 1953
SEE: B68, B234

W128.   *SUITE BOURGEOISE* (1940)
        for flute, trumpet and piano

        I   - Prelude (Moderato)
        II   - Tango (Elaine)   (Andante con moto)
        III   - Dance (censored) (Allegro)
        IV   - Ballad (Andante con moto)
        V   - Valse (Vivace - Allegro)

Written in June 1940 for Richard Adeney, the composer and Betty
Coleman to play.
Duration: 13 minutes
First performance: unable to trace
Unpublished

W129.   *THREE FANTASIES FOR PIANO* (Opus 129 - 1986)

      I   - Lento e Mesto
      II   - Vivace
      III - Andante con moto

      Dedication: Eileen Gilroy
      Duration: 4¼ minutes
      First performance: unable to trace
      Unpublished
      RECORDING: D80

W130.   *THREE PIECES FOR PIANO* (1937)

      I   - Prelude (Moderato)
      II   - Air (Andante contabile)
      III - Gigue (Allegro vivace)

      Duration: c.4 minutes
      First performance: unable to trace
      Unpublished
      RECORDING: D81

W131.   *THREE PIECES FOR PIANO* (1943)

      I   - Prelude (Andante lamentoso)
      II   - Romance (Andante con molto espressivo)
      III - Lament (Andante moderato)

      Duration: c.9 minutes
      First performance: unable to trace
      Unpublished
      RECORDING: D82

W132.   *THREE SHANTIES FOR WIND QUINTET* (Opus 4 - 1943)

      I   - Allegro con brio - Presto
      II   - Allegro semplice
      III - Allegro vivace

      Duration: 6½ minutes
      First performance: Bristol, Filton aerodrome, c. August 1943.
         London Philharmonic Orchestra Wind Quintet

Publication: Paterson, 1952
             Carl Fischer, 1967
RECORDING: D83
SEE: B333

W133.   *TREVELYAN SUITE* (Opus 96 - 1967)
        for 3 flutes, 2 oboes, 2 clarinets, 2 horns and cello (or 2 bassoons)

        I   - Palindrome (Allegro spiritoso)
        II   - Nocturne (Andante con moto)
        III   - Apotheosis (Maestoso)

Written for the opening by Lord Butler of Trevelyan College at the
University of Durham where the composer's daughter was a student.

Duration: 8 minutes
First performance: Durham, Trevelyan College, 12 March 1968.
        University Ensemble, conducted by Malcolm Arnold
Publication: Faber Music, 1970
             Emerson Edition, 1979

W134.   *TRIO FOR FLUTE, VIOLA AND BASSOON* (Opus 6 - 1943)

        I   - Allegro ma non troppo - Presto
        II   - Andante con moto
        III   - Allegro commodo - Andante - Tempo primo

Duration: 10½ minutes
First performance: London, Fyvie Hall, 18 January 1944.
        Richard Adeney (flute), Wrayburn Glasspool (viola) and George
        Alexandra (bassoon)
Publication: Paterson, 1954
SEE: B62, B79, B246

W135.   *TRIO FOR VIOLIN, VIOLA AND PIANO* (Opus 54 - 1956)

        I   - Allegro con fuoco
        II   - Andante
        III   - Vivace energico

Dedication: Pauline Howgill
Duration: 12½ minutes
First performance: London, International Music Association, 30 April

1956.
St Cecilia Trio
Publication: Paterson, 1956
RECORDING: D84
SEE: B285

W136. *TWO BAGATELLES FOR PIANO* (Opus 18 - 1947)

I   - Allegretto
II   - Moderato ma non allegro

Duration: c. 5 minutes
First performance: London, British Music Information Centre, 15 May
      1984. Richard Deering (piano)
Unpublished
RECORDING: D85

W137. *TWO PIECES FOR PIANO* (1941)

I   - Allegro moderato con molto espressivo
II   - Quick

Duration: c. 3 minutes
First performance: unable to trace
Unpublished
RECORDING: D86

W138. *VARIATIONS ON A UKRAINIAN FOLK SONG* (Opus 9 - 1944)
       for solo piano.

Theme (Andante con molto espressivo)
I   - Molto agitato
II   - Allegro vivace
III   - Più Mosso
IV   - Allegretto
V   - Interlude (Andante)
VI   - Vivace
VII   - Allegretto semplice
VIII - Presto
IX   - Andantino cantabile
X   - Fantasia (con fuoco)

Dedication: John Kuchmy [at whose suggestion the variations were
    written]
Duration: 15 minutes
First performance: London, Salle Erard, 19 November 1946.
    Edith Vogel (piano)
Publication: Lengnick, 1948
RECORDING: D88
SEE: B241

V.   CHORAL MUSIC

W139.   *JOHN CLARE CANTATA* (Opus 52 - 1955)
    for mixed chorus and piano duet. Texts by John Clare.

I   - Winter Snow Storm (Andantino)
II   - March (Allegro non troppo)
III   - Spring (Allegretto)
IV   - Summer (Allegro)
V   - Autumn (Andante)
VI   - Epilogue (Andantino)

Commissioned by William Glock for the 1955 Dartington Summer
School of Music
Duration: 11 minutes
First performance: Dartington Hall, Devon, 5 August 1955.
    Summer School Choir with Viola Tunnard and Martin Penny
    (pianos), conducted by John Clements
Publication: Paterson, 1956
SEE: B384

W140.   *JOLLY OLD FRIAR* (1966)
    for unison voices and piano

Text by Frank Richards
Publication: Cassell, 1966 (Greyfriars' School Annual)

W141.   *THE PEACOCK IN THE ZOO* (1963)
    for unison voices and piano

Text: Katherine Arnold
Duration: 2 minutes

First performance: unable to trace
Publication: Paterson, 1963

W142.   *PSALM 150 - LAUDATE DOMINUM* (Opus 25 - 1950
for mixed chorus and organ

Commissioned by St.Matthew's Church, Northampton
Dedication: "To the Revd Canon Walter Hussey, the choir and organist
of St.Matthew's Church, Northampton"
Duration: 7 minutes
First performance: Northampton, St Matthew's Church, 1950.
        Church Choir conducted by Philip Pfaff
Publication: Lengnick, 1950

W143.   *THE RETURN OF ODYSSEUS* (Opus 119 - 1976)
Cantata for mixed chorus and orchestra. Text by Patric Dickinson.

Commissioned by the Schools' Music Association
2.2.2.2/4.3.3.1/timpani percussion (2) harp/strings
Duration: 30 minutes
First performance: London, Royal Albert Hall, 24 April 1977.
        Schools' Music Association Choir with the orchestra of the RCM,
        conducted by David Willcocks
Publication: Faber Music, 1976

W144.   *ST. ENDELLION RINGERS* (1968)
Canon for unaccompanied chorus

Duration: 30 seconds
First performance: unable to trace
Unpublished

W145.   *SONG OF FREEDOM* (Opus 109 - 1972)
for chorus of soprano and altos and brass band

Arnold chose the texts from poems on freedom written by children as
part of a nationwide competition sponsored by the NSBBA, who also
commissioned the work.

| I | - Prelude (Moderato) | Text: Maureen Parr, Nina Truzka, Susan Selwyn |
| II | - Hymn (Risoluto) | Text: Vivienne McClean |

III   - Intermezzo (Lento)   Text: Diana Henry, Caroline
                                                 Richardson, Marianne Porter
IV   - Postlude (Maestoso con moto) Text: John M Thompson,
                                                 Maureen Parr

Dedication: The National Schools Brass Band Association, in
          celebration of the 21st anniversary of its founding
Duration: 19 minutes
First performance: Harrow, Sports Centre, 12 May 1973.
          Nettleswell School Band and Choir, conducted by Malcolm
          Arnold
First London: Royal Albert Hall, 6 October 1973.
          Harrow Schools' Girls Choir with the GUS (Footwear) Band,
          conducted by Geoffrey Brand
Publication: Henrees Music, 1972
          SEE: B380

W146. *SONG OF PRAISE* (Opus 55 - 1956)
       for unison voices and piano, or strings and piano, or orchestra
       Text: John Clare

       Commissioned by Ruth Railton for the jubilee of Wycombe Abbey
       School
       1.1.1.1/2.2.2.0/timpani percussion organ/strings
       Duration: 4 minutes
       First performance: unable to trace
       Publication: Paterson, 1956

W147. *SONG OF SIMEON* (Opus 69 - 1959)
       Nativity masque for mimes, soloists, mixed chorus and orchestra
       Text: Christopher Hassall

       Written for a charity matinée for the Church of St Martin-in-the-Fields
       0.0.0.0/0.3.3.1/timpani percussion (2) celesta harp/strings
       Duration: 29½ minutes
       First performance: London, Drury Lane Theatre, 5 January 1960.
          Nicholas Chagrin and Imogen Hassall (mimes), St Martin's
          Singers with Concert Orchestra, conducted by Malcolm Arnold
       Publication: Oxford University Press, 1960
                    Faber Music, 1986
       RECORDING: D66
       SEE: B225, B336

W148.   *THIS CHRISTMAS NIGHT* (1967)
        for unaccompanied mixed chorus

        Text: Mary Wilson
        Duration: 1½ minutes
        First performance: unable to trace
        Publication: Faber Music, 1968

W149.   *TWO CEREMONIAL PSALMS FOR TREBLE VOICES* (Opus 35 -
        1952)
        Written for Anne Mendoza for performance at her wedding to Philip
        Goldesgeyme

        I   - O come, let us sing (Maestoso)
        II   -Make a joyful noise (Giubiloso)

        Duration: 5 minutes
        First performance: London, Marble Arch Synagogue, January 1952.
        Publication: Paterson, 1952

W150.   *TWO PART-SONGS* (1939)
        for unaccompanied voices. Text by Ernest Dowson

        I   - Spleen (Andante con moto)
        II   - Vitae Summa Brevis Spem Nos Uetat Incohare Longam

        Duration: 1¾ minutes
        First performance: unable to trace
        Unpublished

VI.   VOCAL MUSIC

W151.   *CONTRASTS* (Opus 134 - 1988)
        Serenade for high voice and string orchestra

        I   - Samuel Johnson (Andantino)
        II   - William Blake (Andantino)
        III - Anonymous (Allegro Scherzando)
        IV   - Chikamatsu Monzaemon (Lento)
        V   - Emily Dickinson (Allegretto)

Dedication: For Robert Tear with affection and admiration
Duration: 9 minutes
First performance: Norwich, St Andrew's Hall, 11 April 1989.
>   Robert Tear (tenor) with the City of London Sinfonia, conducted
>   by Richard Hickox
Publication: Novello, 1989

W152.   *FIVE WILLIAM BLAKE SONGS* (Opus 66 - 1959)
for contralto and strings

I   - O Holy Virgin! Clad in purest white (Moderato)
II   - Memory, hither come and tune your merry notes (Allegro)
III   - How sweet I roam'd from field to field (Allegretto)
IV   - My silks and fine array (Andante con moto)
V   - Thou fair-hair'd angel of the evening (Lento)

Dedication: Pamela Bowden [for whom they were written]
Duration: 12½ minutes
First performance: Richmond, Community Centre Hall, 26 March 1959.
>   Pamela Bowden (contralto) with the Richmond Community Centre
>   String Orchestra, conducted by Malcolm Arnold
First London: Victoria and Albert Museum, 12 July 1959.
>   Pamela Bowden with the Jacques Orchestra conducted by
>   Reginald Jacques
Publication: British and Continental Music Agencies, 1966
RECORDING: D33
SEE: B298

W153.   *KENSINGTON GARDENS* (1938)
Song-cycle for medium voice and piano.

I   - Night (Andante con moto)
II   - Tulip (Allegro moderato)
III   - Noon (Andante con moto)
IV   - Daffodil (Andante con moto)
V   - Lupin (Allegretto)
VI   -Hawthorn Tree (Andante)
VII   - The Rose (Presto - Allegretto - Presto - Adagio)
VIII   - Laburnum (Andante moderato)
IX   - The Chestnut and the Beech Tree (Allegretto)

Text: Humbert Wolfe
Duration: 7½ minutes

First performance: unable to trace
Unpublished

W154.   *THE SONG OF ACCOUNTING PERIODS* (Opus 103 - 1969)
for voice and piano

Text: From the 1965 Finance Act
Duration: 2¾ minutes
First performance: London, Purcell Room, 4 May 1969.
        John Godber (tenor) and John Gould (piano)
Unpublished

W155.   *TWO JOHN DONNE SONGS* (Opus 114b - 1974)
for tenor and piano

I   - The Good-Morrow (Andante con moto)
II   - Woman's Constancy (Allegro moderato)

Dedication: "for Niamh"
Duration: 6 minutes
First performance: Bristol, the University, 23 June 1977.
        Ian Partridge (tenor) and Jennifer Partridge (piano)
Publication: Robertson, 1977

W156.   *TWO SONGS FOR VOICE AND PIANO* (Opus 8 - 1944)
for voice and piano

I   - Neglected (Allegro - Andante - Allegro)
        Text: Mei Sheng (tr. A. Waley)
II   - Morning Noon (Andante con moto)
        Text: Mei Sheng (tr. M. Carpenter)

Duration: 5 minutes
First performance: London, Salle Erard, 25 February 1947.
        Joyce Newton (mezzo-soprano) and Mabel Lovering (piano)
Unpublished

VII.   FILM MUSIC

W157.   *AFRICA - TEXAS STYLE* (1966)
        US title: Cowboy in Africa

Director: Andrew Marton
Screenplay: Andy White
4.2.1.0/4.3.3.0/2 guitars/piano/perc (4)/strings
Music: Orchestra/ Malcolm Arnold

W158.   *AIRWAYS* (1950)

Production: John Harvell
Music: Orchestra/John Hollingsworth

W159.   *ALBERT RN* (1953)
US title: Break to Freedom

Director: Lewis Gilbert
Screenplay: Guy Morgan and Vernon Harris
Music: Orchestra/Philip Martel

W160.   *ALIEN ORDERS* (1951)

Production: Crown Film Unit for the Central Office of Information
Music: Orchestra/John Hollingsworth

W161.   *THE ANGRY SILENCE* (1960)

Director: Guy Green
Screenplay: Bryan Forbes
Music: Orchestra/Malcolm Arnold

W162.   *ANTHONY AND CLEOPATRA* (1949)

Music: Philharmonia Orchestra/Malcolm Arnold

W163.   *AVALANCHE PATROL* (1947)

Production: Swiss Avalanche Patrol (GB) - Jack Swain
Director: Jack Swain
Music: London Symphony Orchestra/John Hollingsworth

W164.   *BADGERS GREEN* (1948)

Director: John Irwin
Screenplay: R.C. Sherriff
Music: Orchestra/Muir Mathieson

W165.   *THE BARRETTS OF WIMPOLE STREET* (1956)

Director: Sidney Franklin
Screenplay: John Dighton

Arnold provided the original score and conducted his own music for the film. However this was replaced by music by Bronislau Kaper when the film was released.

W166.   *THE BATTLE OF BRITAIN* (1969)

Director: Guy Hamilton
Screenplay: James Kennaway and Wilfred Greatorex

2+1.2+1.2+1/4.3.3.1/timpani percussion (3) harp/strings

Music: Orchestra/Malcolm Arnold and William Walton (for the March)

N.B. Arnold conducted the majority of the recording sessions at Denham Studios in March/April 1969, and assisted in orchestrating several sections of the music, including the Battle of Britain March. He also rescored and expanded several sections of Walton's original music, including the Battle in the Air sequence, the last third of which he completed.
SEE: B198

W167.   *THE BEAUTIFUL COUNTY OF AYR* (1949)

Production: Anglo-Scottish Films
2.1.2.0/0.2.2.0/percussion harp/strings
Music: Orchestra/James Walker

W168.   *BEAUTIFUL STRANGER* (1954)
US title: Twist of Fate

Director: David Miller
Screenplay: Robert Westerby and Carl Nystrom
Music: Orchestra/Malcolm Arnold

W169.   *THE BELLES OF ST. TRINIAN'S* (1954)

Director: Frank Launder

Screenplay: Frank Launder, Sidney Gilliat and Val Valentine

1.1.1.1/0.2.1.0/percussion (2) piano duet/strings
Music: Orchestra/Malcolm Arnold
SEE: B91

OTHER VERSIONS
(1)   *Suite* - arranged by C. Palmer

Unpublished

W170.   *BLUE MURDER AT ST. TRINIAN'S* (1957)

Director: Frank Launder
Screenplay: Frank Launder, Val Valentine and Sidney Gilliat
Music: Orchestra/Malcolm Arnold
SEE: B91

W171.   *THE BOY AND THE BRIDGE* (1959)

Director: Kevin McClory
Screenplay: Geoffrey Orme, Kevin McClory and Desmond O'Donovan
Music: Orchestra/Malcolm Arnold

W172.   *THE BRIDGE ON THE RIVER KWAI* (1957)

Director: David Lean
Screenplay: Carl Foreman, from the novel by Pierre Boulle
Music: Royal Philharmonic Orchestra/Malcolm Arnold
Versions arrangements published by Columbia Pictures Music
Corporation, New York and Campbell Connelly, London.
SEE: B24, B328, B362

OTHER VERSIONS
(1)   *Suite* - arranged by C. Palmer

Unpublished
RECORDING: D3

W173.   *BRITANNIA MEWS* (1949)
        US tile: The Forbidden Street

        Director: Jean Negulesco

Screenplay: Ring Lardner Jr., from the novel by Margery Sharp
Music: Royal Philharmonic Orchestra/Muir Mathieson

W174.   *THE CAPTAIN'S PARADISE* (1953)

Director: Anthony Kimmins
Screenplay: Alec Coppell and Nicholas Phipps

1.1.2.1/3.2.2.0/timpani percussion (2) guitar piano harp/strings
Music: Orchestra/Muir Mathieson

W175   *THE CHALK GARDEN (1963)*

Director: Ronald Neame
Screenplay: John Michael Hayes, from the novel by Enid Bagnold
Music: Orchestra/Malcolm Arnold
Arrangements published by Henrees Music and Editions Feldman SA

W176.   *CHANNEL ISLANDS* (1952)

Production: British Transport Film
Director: Michael Orrom
Music: Orchestra/Malcolm Arnold

W177.   *CHARTING THE SEAS* (1948)

Director: Harold Lowenstein
Music: Orchestra/John Hollingsworth

W178.   *THE CONSTANT HUSBAND* (1954)

Director: Sidney Gilliat
Screenplay: Sidney Gilliat and Val Valentine
Music: London Philharmonic Orchestra/Muir Mathieson

W179.   *COPENHAGEN, CITY OF TOWERS* (1953)

Production: Fitzpatrick Traveltalk

W180.   *COTTON - LANCASHIRE'S TIME FOR ADVENTURE* (1948)

Production: This Modern Age

W181. *COUPE DES ALPES* (1958)

Production: Shell Film Unit
Director: John Armstrong
Music: Orchestra/Malcolm Arnold

W182. *CURTAIN UP* (1952)

Director: Ralph Smart
Screenplay: Michael Pertwee and Jack Davies from the play "On Monday Next" by Philip King
Music: Orchestra/Muir Mathieson

W183. *DAVID COPPERFIELD* (1969)

Director: Delbert Mann
Screenplay: Jack Pulman, based on the novel by Charles Dickens
Music: Orchestra/Malcolm Arnold
Publication: Twentieth Century Music Corporation, 1970

W184. *THE DEEP BLUE SEA* (1955)

Director: Anatole Litvak
Screenplay: Terence Rattigan
Music: Orchestra/Muir Mathieson

W185. *DEVIL ON HORSEBACK* (1953)

Production: Group Three
Director: Cyril Frankel
Music: Orchestra/Malcolm Arnold

W186. *DOLLARS AND SENSE* (1949)

Production: Crown Film Unit
Director: Diane Pine
Music: Orchestra/John Hollingsworth

W187. *DRUMS FOR A HOLIDAY* (1949)

Production: Anglo-Scottish Films
Director: A.R. Taylor
Music: Orchestra/James Walker

W188.   *DUNKIRK* (1957)

Director: Leslie Norman
Screenplay: W.P. Lipscomb and David Divine
Music: Sinfonia of London/Muir Mathieson

W189.   *ECA PRODUCTIVITY TEAM* (1950)

Details unknown

W190.   *EVWs* (1949)

Production: Data Films for the Central Office of Information
Director: Michael Orrom
Music: Orchestra/John Hollingsworth

W191.   *FIFTY ACRES (*1950)

Production: Green Park
Director: Peter Plaskitt
Music: Orchestra/John Hollingsworth

W192.   *FIGHT FOR A FULLER LIFE* (1949)

Production: This Modern Age

W193.   *FOUR-SIDED TRIANGLE* (1952)

Director: Terence Fisher
Screenplay: Paul Tabori and Terence Fisher, from the novel by
               William F. Temple
Music: Royal Philharmonic Orchestra/Muir Mathieson

W194.   *THE FRAZERS OF CABOT COVE* (1949)

Production: Green Park
Director: Humphrey Swingler
Music: Orchestra/John Hollingsworth

W195.   *GATES OF POWER* (1948)

Production: Anglo-Scottish Film
Director: Anthony Squire

Music: Orchestra/James Walker

W196.   *THE GREAT ST. TRINIAN'S TRAIN ROBBERY* (1964)

Directors: Frank Launder and Sidney Gilliat
Screenplay: Frank Launder and Ivor Herbert

1.1.2.1/1.1.1.0/guitar/percussion (2)/celesta/strings
Music: Orchestra/Malcolm Arnold

W197.   *HAWICK, QUEEN OF THE BORDER* (1948)

Production: Crown Film Unit
Music: Orchestra/John Hollingsworth

W198.   *THE HEROES OF TELEMARK* (1966)

Director: Anthony Mann
Screenplay: Ian Moffat and Ben Barzman
Music: Orchestra/Malcolm Arnold
Publication: Columbia Pictures Music Corporation, 1966

W199.   *A HILL IN KOREA* (1956)
US title: Hell in Korea

Director: Julian Amyes
Screenplay: Ian Dalrymple, Anthony Squire and Ronald Spencer, from
             the novel by Max Catto
Music: Orchestra/Muir Mathieson
SEE: B23

W200.   *HOBSON'S CHOICE* (1953)

Director: David Lean
Screenplay: Norman Spencer and Wynyard Browne, from the play by
             Harold Brighouse
Music: Royal Philharmonic Orchestra/Muir Mathieson
Publication: Paterson, 1954
SEE: B328

OTHER VERSIONS
(1)   *Suite* - arranged by C. Palmer

Unpublished
RECORDING: D41

(2)   *Hobson's Choice*: excerpts arranged for string trio by Leslie A. Hogan

Duration: 15 minutes
Unpublished
RECORDING: D41

W201.   *THE HOLLY AND THE IVY* (1952)

Director: George More O'Ferrall
Screenplay: Anatole de Grunwald, from the play by Wynyard Browne
Music: Royal Philharmonic Orchestra/Muir Mathieson

OTHER VERSIONS
(1)   *Fantasy on Chrsitmas Carols* (The Holly and the Ivy) - arranged
        by C. Palmer
RECORDING: D42

W202.   *HOME AT SEVEN* (1951)
US title: Murder on Monday

Director: Ralph Richardson
Screenplay: Anatole de Grunwald from the play by R.C. Sherriff
Music: Orchestra/Muir Mathieson

W203   *HOME TO DANGER* (1951)

Director: Terence Fisher
Music: Orchestra/Muir Mathieson

W204.   *HYDROGRAPHY* (1948)

Details unknown

W205.   *I AM A CAMERA* (1955)

Director: Henry Cornelius
Screenplay: John Collier
Music: Orchestra/Muir Mathieson

W206. *THE INN OF THE SIXTH HAPPINESS* (1958)

    Director: Mark Robson
    Screenplay: Isobel Lennart, from the book "The Small Woman" by Alan Burgess

    0.1.0.0/1.0.0.0/guitar percussion (2) celesta harp/strings
    Music: Royal Philharmonic Orchestra/Malcolm Arnold
    Publication: B. Feldman & Co. 1958 and 1961

    OTHER VERSIONS
    (1)   *Suite* - arranged by C. Palmer

    Unpublished
    RECORDING: D44

W207. *THE INSPECTOR* (1962)
    US title: Lisa

    Director: Philip Dunne
    Screenplay: Nelson Gidding, for the novel by Jan de Hartog
    Music: Orchestra/Malcolm Arnold
    Publication: Henrees Music, 1962

W208. *INVITATION TO THE DANCE* (1952)

    Director and Choreographer: Gene Kelly
    Music: Orchestra/John Hollingsworth
    Written in collaboration with Jacques Ibert

W209. *THE ISLAND* (1952)

    Production: Data Films
    Directors: Peter Pickering, John Ingram
    Music: Orchestra/John Hollingsworth

W210. *ISLAND IN THE SUN (1957)*

    Director: Robert Rossen
    Screenplay: Alfred Hayes, from the novel by Alec Waugh
    Music: Royal Philharmonic Orchestra/Malcolm Arnold
    Publication: Robbins Music Corporation, 1957

W211. *IT STARTED IN PARADISE* (1952)

Director: Compton Bennett
Screenplay: Marghanita Laski
Music: Orchestra/Muir Mathieson
Publication: Paterson, 1952

W212. *JULIUS CAESAR* (1949)

Music: Philharmonia Orchestra/Malcolm Arnold

W213. *THE KEY* (1958)

Director: Carol Reed
Screenplay: Carl Foreman, from the novel "Stella" by Jan de Hartog
Music: Orchestra/Muir Mathieson
Publication: Columbia Pictures Music Corporation and Campbell
              Connelly, 1958

W214. *LET GO FOR 'ARD* (1950)

Production: Anglo-American Oil
Music: Orchestra/Malcolm Arnold

W215. *THE LION* (1962)

Director: Jack Cardiff
Screenplay: Irene and Louis Kamp, from the novel by Joseph Kessel
Music: Orchestra/Malcolm Arnold
Publication: Henrees Music, 1962

W216. *LOCAL NEWSPAPERS* (1951)

Production: Crown Film Unit
Music: Orchestra/John Hollingsworth

W217. *MAN OF AFRICA* (1953)

Director: Cyril Frankel
Screenplay: Montagu Slater
Music: Orchestra/Malcolm Arnold

W218. *MEN AND MACHINES* (1951)

Production: Wessex films
Music: Orchestra/Malcolm Arnold

W219.   *METROPOLITAN WATER BOARD* (1948)

Production: World Wide Films
Music: Orchestra/John Hollingsworth

W220.   *MINING REVIEW* (1948)

Production: Data films for the Central Office of Information
Director: Michael Orrom
Music: Orchestra/Malcolm Arnold

W221.   *THE NIGHT MY NUMBER CAME UP* (1955)

Director: Leslie Norman
Screenplay: R.C. Sherriff
2.2.2+1.1/4.3.2+1.1/timpani percussion (2) celesta harp/strings
Music: London Symphony Orchestra/Muir Mathieson

W222.   *NINE HOURS TO RAMA* (1962)

Director: Mark Robson
Screenplay: Nelson Gidding, from the novel by Stanley Wolpert
Music: Orchestra/Malcolm Arnold
Publication: Henrees Music, 1963

W223.   *1984* (1955)

Director: Michael Anderson
Screenplay: William P. Templeton and Ralph Bettinson, from the
                novel by George Orwell
Music: London Symphony Orchestra/Louis Levy

W224.   *NO HIGHWAY* (1951)
        US title: No Highway in the Sky

Director: Henry Koster
Screenplay: R. C. Sherriff, Oscar Millard and Alec Coppel, based on
                the novel by Neville Shute
Music: Orchestra/Marcus Dods

W225.   *NO LOVE FOR JOHNNIE* (1960)

Director: Ralph Thomas
Screenplay: Nicholas Phipps and Mordecai Richler, from the novel by
                 Wilfred Fienburgh

Music: Orchestra/Malcolm Arnold
Publication: Film Music Publishing, 1961

W226.   *NORTH SEA STRIKE* (1967)

Production: Gerald Holdsworth Productions
Director: Dan Kelly
Music: Orchestra/Malcolm Arnold

W227.   *OIL REVIEW NO. 5* (1950)

Production: Green Park
Music: Orchestra/John Hollingsworth

W228.   *ON THE FIDDLE* (1961)
          US title: Operation Snafu

Director: Cyril Frankel
Screenplay: Harold Buchman, for the novel "Stop at a Winner"
                 by R.F. Delderfield
Music: Orchestra/Malcolm Arnold
Publication: Henrees Music, 1961

W229.   *PORT AFRIQUE* (1956)

Director: Rudolph Maté
Screenplay: Frank Patos and John Cresswell, from the novel by
                 Bernard Vieter Dryer
Music: Orchestra/Muir Mathieson

W230.   *POWER FOR ALL* (1951)

Production: Wessex Films
Directors: Graham Wallace, Anthony Squire
Music: Orchestra/Malcolm Arnold

W231.   *POWERED FLIGHT: THE STORY OF THE CENTURY* (1953)

Production: Shell Film Unit (GB) - Stuart Legg
Music: Orchestra/Malcolm Arnold

W232. *A PRIZE OF GOLD* (1954)

Director: Mark Robson
Screenplay: Robert Buckner and John Paxton, from the novel by Max
            Catto
Music: Orchestra/Muir Mathieson

W233. *THE PURE HELL OF ST. TRINIAN'S* (1960)

Director: Frank Launder
Screenplay: Frank Launder, Val Valentine and Sidney Gilliat
Music: Orchestra/Malcolm Arnold

W234. *THE RECKONING* (1969)

Director: Jack Gold
Screenplay: John McGrath, from the novel "The Harp that Once" by
            Patrick Hall
Music: Orchestra/Malcolm Arnold

W235. *REPORT ON STEEL* (1948)

Production: Data films of Central Office of Information
Director: Michael Orrom
Music: Orchestra/John Hollingsworth

OTHER VERSIONS
(1) *Symphonic Study: Machines* (Opus 30 - 1951)
for brass, percussion and strings

0.0.0.0/4.3.3.1/timpani percussion (2)/strings

Theme (Allegro commodo)
I   - Vivace
II   - Andante
III   - Allegro con brio
IV   - [Allegro con brio]
V   - Allegro commodo - Lento e maestoso

Duration: 6 minutes

First performance: Glasgow, Henry Wood Hall, 5 October 1984.
  BBC Scottish Orchestra, conducted by Charles Groves
Publication: Faber Music, 1984

W236.   *THE RIDDLE OF JAPAN* (1950)

Production: This Modern Age
4.1.1.0/4.2.2.0/timpani percussion (2) prio harp/strings (cellos and
  double basses only)

W237.   *THE RINGER* (1952)

Director: Guy Hamilton
Screenplay: Val Valentine, for the novel by Edgar Wallace
Music: Orchestra/Muir Mathieson

W238.   *THE ROOTS OF HEAVEN* (1958)

Director: John Huston
Screenplay: Romain Gary and Patrick Leigh-Fermor, for the novel by
               Romain Gary
2.2.2.1+1/4.3.3.1/timpani percussion piano harp/strings (8 7 6 5 4)
Music: Orchestra/Malcolm Arnold

W239.   *ROSES TATTOO* (1956)

Production: Anglo - Scottish Pictures
Music: Orchestra/James Walker

W240.   *THE ROYAL TOUR - NEW ZEALAND* (1954)

Production: Patré Documentary Unit (GB) - Howard Thomas
Music: Orchestra/Muir Mathieson

W241.   *SCIENCE OF THE ORCHESTRA* (1949)

Production: Realist Films
Director: Alec Strasser
Music: Orchestra/Muir Mathieson

W242.   *THE SEA SHALL NOT HAVE THEM* (1954)

Director: Lewis Gilbert
Screenplay: Lewis Gilbert and Vernon Harris
Music: Orchestra/Muir Mathieson

W243.   *SEVEN RAF FLASHES* (1947)

Production: Cavalier Film
Music: Orchestra/John Hollingsworth

W244.   *SKY WEST AND CROOKED* (1966)
US title: Gypsy Girl

Director: John Mills
Screenplay: Mary Hayley Bell and John Prebble
Music: Orchestra/Malcolm Arnold
Publication: Henreas Music, 1966

W245.   *THE SLEEPING TIGER* (1954)

Director: Joseph Losey
Screenplay: Harold Buchman and Carl Foreman, from the novel by
                   Maurice Moiseiwitch
Music: Orchestra/Music Mathieson

W246.   *SOLOMON AND SHEBA* (1959)
- Funeral March Sequence

Director: King Vidor
Screenplay: Anthony Veiller, Paul Dudley and George Bruce

W247.   *THE SOUND BARRIER* (1952)
US title: Breaking the Sound Barrier

Director: David Lean
Screenplay: Terence Rattigan
Music: Royal Philharmonic Orchestra/Muir Mathieson
SEE: B74, B328

OTHER VERSIONS
(1)   *The Sound Barrier* (Opus 38 - 1952)
Rhapsody for orchestra

3.2.2.2/4.3.3.1/timpani percussion (2) celesta harp/strings

Duration: 7½ minutes
First performance: BBC Radio 3, 23 May 1984.
      Ulster Orchestra, conducted by Yannis Daras
Publication: Paterson, 1952
RECORDING: D67

(2)   *The Sound Barrier*
Arranged for wind band

First performance: Chicago (USA), 20 December 1995.
First European and UK performance: Basingstoke, The Anvil,
      10 February 1996.
      The Inns of Court and City Yeomanry Band; The Scots Guards;
      Lanalee de Kant Montgomery (harp), conducted by Rodney Parker
Unpublished

W248.   *STOLEN FACE* (1952)

Director: Terence Fisher
Screenplay: Martin Berkley and Richard H. Lanau

3.2+1.2.2/4.3.3.0/timpani percussion harp/strings/solo piano
Music: Orchestra/Malcolm Arnold

W249.   *THE STORY OF GILBERT AND SULLIVAN* (1953)
      US title: The Great Gilbert and Sullivan

Director: Sidney Gilliat
Screenplay: Sidney Gilliat and Leslie Bailey
Music: Orchestra/Malcolm Sargent

W250.   *THE STRUGGLE FOR OIL* (1948)

Production: This Modern Age
4.2.2 + asax.0/4.3.3.1/timpani percussion (2) harp/strings

W251.   *SUDDENLY LAST SUMMER* (1959)

Director: Joseph L. Mankiewicz
Screenplay: Gore Vidal, for the play by Tennessee Williams
Music: Orchestra/Buxton Orr

W252.   *TAMAHINE* (1963)

Director: Philip Leacock
Screenplay: Dennis Cannan, from the novel by Thelma Niklaus

1.1.2+1.0/3.2.1.0/Hawaiian guitar percussion (3) celesta harp/strings, together with wind and brass group for the Concert Band Sequence
Music: Orchestra/Malcolm Arnold
Publication: Harms Witmark, London, 1963

W253. *TERRA INCOGNITA* (1949)

Production: Verity
Music: Orchestra/Malcolm Arnold

W254. *THE THIN RED LINE* (1964)

Director: Andrew Marton
Screenplay: Bernard Gordon, from the novel by James Jones
Music: Orchestra/Malcolm Arnold

W255. *THIS FARMING BUSINESS* (1949)

Production: Green Park
Music: Orchestra/John Hollingsworth

W256. *THIS IS BRITAIN* (1950)

Production: Crown Film Unit
Music: Orchestra/John Hollingsworth

W257. *TIGER IN THE SMOKE* (1956)

Director: Roy Baker
Screenplay: Anthony Pelissier, from the novel by Marjorie Allingham
Music: Orchestra/Malcolm Arnold

W258. *TRAPEZE* (1956)

Director: Carol Reed
Screenplay: James R. Webb
Music: Orchestra/Muir Mathieson
Publication: Cromwell Music and Essex Music, 1956

W259. *TRIESTE: PROBLEM CITY (1949)*

Production: This Modern Age

W260.   *TUNES OF GLORY* (1960)

Director: Ronald Neame
Screenplay: James Kennaway, from his novel
1+1.1.3+1.0/4.3.3.1/timpani percussion (2) harp piano/strings
Music: Orchestra/Malcolm Arnold
Publication: United Artists Music Ltd., 1960 and 1961

W261.   *TWO RAF FLASHES* (1948)

Production: Cavalier Films
Music: Orchestra/John Hollingsworth

W262.   *UP FOR THE CUP* (1950)

Director: Jack Raymond
Screenplay: Jack Marks and Con West

Percival Mackey composed most of the score, but Arnold scored several
of the longer sequences

W263.   *VALUE FOR MONEY* (1955)

Director: Ken Annakin
Screenplay: R. F. Delderfield and William Fairchild, from the novel by
                    Derrick Boothroyd
Music: Orchestra/Muir Mathieson

W264.   *WELCOME THE QUEEN* (1954)

Production: Patné Documentary Unit
Music: Orchestra/Muir Mathieson

W265.   *WHEN YOU WENT AWAY* (1949)

Production: This Modern Age

W266.   *WHERE BRITAIN STANDS* (1950)

Production: This Modern Age

W267.   *WHISTLE DOWN THE WIND* (1961)

Director: Bryan Forbes
Screenplay: Keith Waterhouse and Willis Hall, from the novel by Mary
                    Hayley Bell
Music: Orchestra/Malcolm Arnold
Publication: Henrees Music, 1961
                    B Feldman & Co

OTHER VERSIONS
(1)   *Suite* - arranged by C. Palmer

Unpublished
RECORDING: D90

W268.   *WICKED AS THEY COME* (1956)
US title: Portrait in Smoke

Director: Ken Hughes
Screenplay: Ken Hughes, Robert Westerby and Sigmund Miller
Music: Sinfonia of London/Muir Mathieson

W269.   *THE WILDCATS OF ST.TRINIAN'S* (1980)

Director: Frank Launder
Screenplay: Frank Launder

Music composed by J. K. Clarke, with music by Arnold from earlier St.
Trinian's films

W270.   *WINGS OF DANGER* (1951)

Director: Terence Fisher
Music: London Philharmonic Orchestra/Malcolm Arnold

W271.   *THE WOMAN FOR JOE* (1955)

Director: George More O'Ferrall
Screenplay: Neil Paterson
Music: Orchestra/Muir Mathieson

W272.   *WOMEN IN OUR TIME* (1948)

Production: This Modern Age

2.1.2+ asax.0 /4.2.2.0/timpani percussion piano harp/strings (6 4 3 2 1)
together with women's voices
Music: London Symphony Orchestra/Muir Mathieson

W273.   *YOU KNOW WHAT SAILORS ARE* (1953)

Director: Ken Annakin
Screenplay: Peter Rogers

3.2.2.1/4.3.3.1/timpani percussion (2) harp/strings
Music: Orchestra/Muir Mathieson

OTHER VERSIONS
(1)   *Scherzetto*: arranged for clarinet and orchestra by C. Palmer
Unpublished
RECORDING: D91

W274.   *YOUR WITNESS* (1949)
        US title: Eye Witness

Director: Robert Montgomery
Screenplay: Hugo Butler, Ian Hunter and William Douglas Home
Music: Orchestra/John Hollingsworth

VIII.   INCIDENTAL MUSIC

W275.   *CANDLEMAS NIGHT* (1955)
        Incidental music for Ernest Reynolds' radio play
        Produced by Frederick Bradnum

Piccolo, 2 flutes, trumpet, timpani, percussion, harp and celesta

Duration of music: 15 minutes
First performance: Broadcast in BBC Third Programme, 25 De-
                     cember 1955.
                     Music played by chamber ensemble, conducted by Lionel
                     Salter (pre-recorded) 18 November 1955
Unpublished

W276.   *ELECTRA* (1955)
Incidental music for Sophocles' play
Produced by Thomas Vaughan and Donald Bisset

I   - Prelude (Poco lento e espressivo)
II   - Electra's Entrance (Andantino ma agitato)
III   - Lento alla marcia funerale
IV   - Lento e misterioso
V   - Postlude (Moderato ma non troppo allegro)

Flute and percussion

First performance: London, Edric Hall (Borough Polytechnic), 7
        December 1955.
        Music played by Christopher Hyde-Smith (flute) and James
        Wolfenden (percussion)
Unpublished

W277.   *ESPIONAGE* (1963)
Music for the ATV television series: music for 14 episodes
Executive producer: Herbert Hirschman

1+1.1+1.1.0/2.1.2.1/guitar percussion harp piano/strings

Duration: Varies for each episode
First performance/transmission: 5 October 1963.
Unpublished

W278.   *FANFARE - ABC TV TITLE MUSIC* (1956)
Written to launch the ABC TV Network

Duration: 1½ minutes
First performance: unable to trace
        Orchestra conducted by Muir Mathieson
Unpublished

W279.   *THE FIRST LADY* (1968)
Opening and closing titles for the BBC TV series
Produced by David E. Rose

Main titles (Allegro-vivace-meno mosso-allegro)
End titles   (Moderato - allegro)

0.0.0.0/0 picc.trpt.+2.3.1/percussion (2) celesta harp (2)/mixed chorus

Duration: 2¼ minutes
First performance/transmission: 7 April 1968.
Unpublished

W280.   *FOR MR PYE AN ISLAND* (1957)
Incidental music for Mervyn Peake's radio play
Produced by Francis Dillon

2 flutes, clarinet, bass clarinet, trumpet, percussion, harp, piano, celesta
and double bass

Duration of music: 12 minutes
First performance: Broadcast in the BBC Home Service, 10 July 1957.
        Music played by chamber ensemble, conducted by Malcolm Arnold
Unpublished

W281.   *GALA PERFORMANCE* (1963)
Signature tune for the BBC TV series

Main titles (Allegro vivace)
End titles   (Allegro vivace)

2.2.2.2/4.2.3.1./guitar timpani.percussion (2) harp/strings

Duration: 1½ minutes
First performance/transmission: 19 November 1963 (pre-recorded 27
                October 1963.
Orchestra conducted by Malcolm Arnold
Unpublished

W282.   *HARD TIMES* (1977)
Theme music for ITV adaptation of Charles Dickens' novel

3 flutes, clarinet, 2 horns, 3 trumpets, 3 trombones, timpani, percussion

Duration: Unable to trace
First performance/transmission: 25 October 1977 (Granada TV).
        Ensemble conducted by Marcus Dods
Unpublished

W283. *MUSIC FOR YOU* (1959)
Signature tune for the BBC TV series, 1959-61

2+1.2.2.2+1/4.3.3.1/timpani percussion harp/strings

Duration: 2½ minutes
First performance/transmission: 22 March 1959.
Unpublished

W284. *PADDY'S NIGHTMARE* (1954)
Revue number written for the Laurier Lister entertainment, *Joyce Grenfall Requests the Pleasure*

Violin, viola, cello, double bass, clarinet/saxophone trumpet drums piano

First performance: London, Fortune Theatre, 2 June 1954.
Paddy Stone and the Theatre Orchestra, conducted by William Blezard
Unpublished

W285. *PARASOL* (1960)
A musical for television, commissioned by the BBC.
Written by Caryl Brahms and Ned Sherrin, based on the "Anatol" dialogues by Arthur Schnitzler. Produced by Ned Sherrin, with musical numbers staged by Alfred Rodrigues

Duration: 53½ minutes
Transmission date: 20 March 1960 (pre-recorded 18 March 1960).
Music played by the Eric Robinson Orchestra, conducted by Marcus Dods
Publication: B. Feldman & Co., 1961 (vocal album)

W286. *PURPLE DUST* (1953)
Incidental music for Sean O'Casey's play
Produced by Sam Wanamaker

Flute, harp, percussion, string quartet

First performance: Glasgow, Theatre Royal, April 1953.
Unpublished

W287. *ROYAL PROLOGUE* (1957)
Music for television feature, written by Christopher Hassall

Produced by Rex Moorfoot

1.1.2.0/1.2.1.0/timpani percussion harp piano/strings

Duration: 21 minutes
First performance/transmission: 25 December 1957 in a programme
Christmas Round The World.
    Royal Philharmonic Orchestra, conducted by Malcolm Arnold with
    trumpeters of the RMSM (Kneller Hall), conducted by Lt. Col.
    David McBain and an organ solo played by William McKie
    (Westminster Abbey)
Unpublished

W288.   *THE TEMPEST* (1954)
    Incidental music for William Shakespeare's play
    Produced by Robert Helpmann

    Oboe, clarinet, trumpet, harp, glockenspiel, celesta or vibraphone,
    timpani and percussion

    First performance: London, Old Vic Theatre, 13 April 1954.
        Music played by the Old Vic Theatre Orchestra, conducted by
        Christopher Whelan
    Publication: Paterson, 1959
    SEE: B381

W289.   *THEME FOR PLAYER'S* (1965)
    Written for John Player Tobacco as a TV advertising theme but never
    used

    Duration: 24 seconds
    Unpublished

    OTHER VERSIONS
    (1) *Theme pour mon amis*: version for whistler and piano
    Duration: 1 minute
    Unpublished

W290.   *THE TURTLE DRUM* (Opus 92 - 1967)
    A children's play for television (originally entitled *Kaisoo the Fisherboy*)

    Commissioned by the BBC. Produced by John Hosier

1. The Turtle Drum
2. Go back where you belong
3. Round of welcome
4. Divertissement of the deep
5. The four seasons
6. Sayonara song

Flute, piccolo, trumpet, guitar(s), percussion, doublebass

First performance: BBC TV, 26 April 1967 (*Making Music*).
James Blades (percussion) and Livingstone Primary School
Publication: Oxford University Press, 1968
Faber Music, 1986

W291. *WAR IN THE AIR* (1954)
Music for three episodes of the BBC TV series. Written and produced
by John Elliot

1. The Fated Sky: televised 8 November 1954
(pre-recorded 12/13 October)
2. Maximum Effort: televised 29 November 1954
3. Operation Overlord: televised 10 January 1955

2.1.2.1/4.3.3.1/timpani percussion/strings (for The Fated Sky)

Music played by the London Symphony Orchestra, conducted by Muir
Mathieson
Unpublished
SEE: B106

IX. MUSIC FOR BRASS, MILITARY AND WIND ENSEMBLES

W292. *DIVERTIMENTO FOR WIND OCTET* [2 oboes, 2 Bb clarinets, 2
bassoons,2 horns] (Opus 137 - 1988)

I   - Allegro
II   - Larghetto
III - Vivace
IV   - Allegro
V   - Alla Marziale

Commissioned for Camerata Wind soloists with financial assistance for
Northwest Arts
Dedication: To Janet Hilton
Duration: 18 minutes
First performance: Manchester, Royal Northern College of Music, 17
    February 1990.
    Camerata Wind soloists, directed by Janet Hilton
Publication: Novello, 1989

W293.   *FANFARE FOR A FESTIVAL* (1955)
    for brass and percussion

Written for the Hastings Festival
0.0.0.0/4.3+cnt.3.1/timpani percussion (3)
Duration: 2 minutes
First performance: unable to trace
Publication: Studio Music, 1986

W294.   *FANFARE FOR A ROYAL OCCASION* (1956)
    for brass

3 trumpets and 3 trombones
Duration: 1½ minutes
First performance: London, Royal Festival Hall, 19 November 1956
    Trumpeters of the RMSM (Kneller Hall), conducted by Lt.-Col.
    David McBain
Publication: Studio Music, 1986

W295.   *FANFARE FOR LOUIS* (1970)
    for 2 trumpets in Bb

Dedication: for "Louis Armstrong's 70th birthday with admiration and
gratitude"
Duration: 1½ minutes
First performance: London, Queen Elizabeth Hall, 4 July 1970.
    Elgar Howarth and Stanley Woods (trumpets) (Louis Armstrong's
    70th birthday concert)
Publication: Studio Music, 1986
RECORDING: D25

W296.   *FANFARE FOR ONE, 80 YEARS YOUNG* (1971)
    for trumpet

Written to celebrate the 80th birthday of Sir Arthur Bliss in 1971, this fanfare was commissioned by the Council and Chairman of the Composers' Guild of which Sir Arthur was President. Besides Arnold, William Alwyn, Lennox Berkeley, Benjamin Britten, Alan Bush, Geoffrey Bush, Arnold Cooke, Stephen Dodgson, Joseph Horowitz, Elizabeth Maconchy, Edmund Rubbra, Humphrey Searle, Graham Whettam and Grace Williams were among others who contributed musical birthday greetings.

Dedication: To Sir Arthur Bliss with admiration respect and affection
Unpublished

W297.   *[FANFARE FOR THE FARNHAM FESTIVAL]* (1961)
For brass and percussion

5 horns, 6 Bb trumpets, 5 trombones, tuba, cymbals and timpani
Duration: c. 2 minutes
First performance: unable to trace. It is possible that the fanfare was
        played by the members of Tiffin School orchestra at the opening
        concert of the festival in May 1961.
Unpublished

W298.   *FANTASY FOR BRASS BAND* (Opus 114a - 1973)
Written for the 1974 National Brass Band Championships

I   - Prelude (Allegro moderato)
II   - Dance (Allegretto)
III   - Elegy (Andante con moto)
IV   - Scherzo (Vivace)
V   - Postlude (Allegro moderato - Vivace)

Dedication: Tony Giles
Duration: 10 minutes
First performance: London, Royal Albert Hall, 5 October 1974.
        Cory Band, conducted by Maj. H.A. Kenney
Publication: Henrees Music, 1974
RECORDING: D27
SEE: B132

W299.   *FLOURISH FOR A BATTLE* (Opus 139 - 1990)
for wind and brass

Commissioned   by   the   Royal   Air   Force   Benevolent   Fund   to

commemorate the 50th anniversary of the Battle of Britain
Dedication: The RAF Benevolent Fund's 50th Anniversary of the Battle
          of Britain Appeal
Duration: 10 minutes
First performance: London, Royal Festival Hall, 6 April 1990.
          RAF Band, conducted by Wing Commander Barrie Hingley
Publication: Novello, 1990
SEE: B26

W300.   *FLOURISH FOR A 21ST BIRTHDAY* (Opus 44 - 1953)
        for brass and percussion

        Dedication: "To Sir Adrian Boult and the LPO in celebration of the 21st
                  anniversary of the foundation of the orchestra"
        Duration: 3 minutes
        First performance: London, Royal Albert Hall, 7 October 1963.
                  London Philharmonic Orchestra, conducted by Adrian Boult
        Publication: Studio Music, 1986
        SEE: 295

W301.   *HRH THE DUKE OF CAMBRIDGE* (Opus 60 - 1957)
        March for military band

        Written to celebrate the Royal Military School of Music's centenary in
              1957.
        Dedication: Lt.-Co. David McBain
        Duration: 3½ minutes
        First performance: Twickenham, Kneller Hall, 28 June 1957
                  Band of the RMSM (Kneller Hall), conducted by Rodney Bashford
        Publication: Paterson and Carl Fischer, 1957
        RECORDING: D40

W302.   *A HOFFNUNG FANFARE* (1960)
        for brass and percussion

        Written for the Hoftnung Memorial Concert
        Duration: 2 minutes
        First performance: London, Royal Festival Hall, 31 October 1960.
                  Trumpeters of the RMSM (Kneller Hall)
        Unpublished

W303.   *KINGSTON FANFARE* (1959)
        for 3 trumpets and 3 trombones

Duration: 25 seconds
First performance: unable to trace
Publication: Studio Music, 1986

W304. *LITTLE SUITE [No.1] FOR BRASS BAND* (Opus 80 - 1963)

I   - Prelude (Allegro ma non troppo)
II - Siciliano (Andantino)
III - Rondo (Allegro vivace - Presto)

Commissioned by the Scottish Amateur Music Association for the
National Youth Brass Band of Scotland
Duration: 10 minutes
First performance: Aberdeen, High School for Girls, July 1963.
    National Youth Brass Band of Scotland, conducted by Bryden
    Thomson
Publication: Paterson, 1965
RECORDING: D46

W305. *LITTLE SUITE [NO. 2] FOR BRASS BAND* (Opus 93 - 1967)

I   - Round (Allegro molto e ritmico)
II - Cavatina (Andante con moto)
III - Galop (Presto)

Commissioned by the Cornwall Youth Band
Duration: 8¾ minutes
First performance: Cornwall, unable to trace venue, 26 March 1967.
    Cornwall Youth Band, conducted by Malcolm Arnold
Publication: Henrees Music, 1967
RECORDING: D47
SEE: B284

W306. *LITTLE SUITE [NO. 3] FOR BRASS BAND* (Opus 131 - 1987)

I   - Giubiloso
II - Allegretto
III - Vivace

Commissioned by Keith Wilson, Head of Performing Arts and Media
Studies at Salford College of Technology for the college brass band and
first performed on the occasion of the L.S. Lowry Centenary Festival
organised by the City of Salford

Duration: 10 minutes
First performance: Salford, Maxwell Hall (now Salford University), unable to ascertain any date.
Salford College of Technology's Brass Band, conducted by Malcolm Arnold
Publication: Studio Music, 1988

W307.   *MARCH: OVERSEAS* (Opus 70 - 1960)
for military band

Commissioned by the Central Office of Information for the British Trade Fair, New York, in 1960.
Duration: 2½ minutes
First performance: New York, 1960. Unable to trace performers
Publication: Paterson and Carl Fischer, 1960
RECORDING: D51

W308.   *THE PADSTOW LIFEBOAT* (Opus 94 - 1967)
March for brass band

Duration: 4½ minutes
First performance: London, Royal Festival Hall, 10 June 1967.
Black Dyke Mills Band and B.M.C. Band, conducted by Malcolm Arnold
Publication: Henrees Music, 1967
RECORDING: D52

OTHER VERSIONS
(1) *The Padstow Lifeboat March* arranged for military band (Woodfield)
Publication: Henrees Music, 1967

W309.   *QUINTET FOR BRASS* (Opus 73 - 1960)
for 2 trumpets, horn, trombone and tuba

I   - Allegro vivace
II   - Chaconne (Andante com moto)
III   - Con brio

Written for the New York Brass Quintet
Dedication: New York Brass Quintet

Duration: 13 minutes
First performance: New York, 1961.
     New York Brass Quintet
First British: London, St Pancras Festival, 17 March 1962.
     Francis Chagrin Ensemble
Publication: Paterson, 1961
SEE: B218, B221

W310.   *QUINTET [NO. 2] FOR BRASS* (Opus 132 - 1987)

      I   - Vivace
      II   - Lento/Mesto
      III - Vivace

      Commissioned by the Fine Arts Brass Ensemble with funds provided by
      British Reserve Insurance Ltd.
      Dedication: For the Fine Arts Ensemble
      Duration: c. 7 - 8 minutes
      First performance: Cheltenham, Pittville Pump Room, 11 July 1988.
           Fine Arts Brass Ensemble
      Publication: Faber Music, 1988

W311.   *RAILWAY FANFARE* (1975)
      for 6 fanfare trumpets

      Written for the 150th anniversary of railways in Britain
      Duration: 1½ minutes
      First performance: unable to trace
      Publication: Studio Music, 1986
      SEE: B11

W312.   *RICHMOND* (1957)
      fanfare for 3 trumpets and 3 trombones

      Commissioned by the BBC as part of the Royal Prologue music of the
      1957 *Christmas Round the World* programme
      Duration: 36 seconds
      First performance: Richmond (Surrey), Christmas 1957.
           Trumpeters of the RMSM (Kneller Hall), conducted by Rodney
           Bashford.
      Publication: Studio Music, 1986

W313.   *SAVILE CENTENARY FANFARE* (1968)

for 2 B-flat trumpets

Written to celebrate the centenary of the Savile Club, London
Duration: c. 1 minute
First Performance: London, Ballroom of the Savile Club, 30 October
    1968. Two trumpeters from the Brigade of Guards.
Unpublished

W314.   *SYMPHONY FOR BRASS* (Opus 123 - 1978)
    for piccolo trumpet, 3 tpt, horn, 3 tenor trmbs, bass trombone and tuba

    I   - Allegro moderato - Vivace - Tempo primo
    II   - Allegretto grazioso
    III   - Andante con moto
    IV   - Allegro con brio

Dedication: To Philip Jones on his 50th birthday
Duration: 30½ minutes
First performance: Cheltenham, Town Hall, 8 July 1979.
    Philip Jones Brass Ensemble conducted by Howard Snell
First London: Queen Elizabeth Hall, 16 March 1980.   Philip Jones Brass

Ensemble conducted by Howard Snell
Publication: Faber Music, 1978
SEE: B249, B296

W315.   *WATER MUSIC* (Opus 82 - 1964)
    for wind and percussion

    I   - Allegro Maestoso
    II   - Andantino
    III   - Vivace

Written for the National Trust in celebration of the opening of the
Stratford Canal.
Duration: 10 minutes
First performance: Stratford-upon-Avon, a barge moored behind the
    Shakespeare Memorial Theatre, 11 July 1964.
    Ensemble, conducted by Brian Priestman
First concert performance: Manchester, RNCM, 3 November 1984,
    RNCM Wind Ensemble, conducted by Clark Rundell
Unpublished
RECORDING: D89

OTHER VERSIONS
(1) *WATER MUSIC* (Opus 82b): arranged for full orchestra

2+1.2.2.2/4.3.3.1/timpani percussion (2)/strings

First performance: Manchester, Free Trade Hall, 21 March 1965.
Hallé Orchestra, conducted by Lawrence Leonard
Publication: Paterson, 1965

X.   ARRANGEMENTS OF MUSIC BY OTHER COMPOSERS

W316.   *CHRISTMAS CAROLS* (1960)
Written and arranged for the Save the Children Fund

1.   The First Nowell (Allegretto): arr. guitar, baritone, chorus and
orchestra
2.2.2.2/4.2.3.1/timpani percussion (2) celesta harp/strings
2.   Away in a Manger (Moderato): arr. orchestra
2.1.2.1/4.0.0.0/glock.cel.harp/strings
3.   Good King Wenceslas (Allegro moderato): arr. brass band and
orchestra
2.1.2.1/4.2.2.1/percussion piano harp/strings

First performance: London, St Martin-in-the-Fields, 19 December
1960.
Unable to trace performance.
Unpublished

OTHER VERSIONS
(1) *Fantasy on Christmas Carols*
arranged by C. Palmer
RECORDING: D42

W317.   *DOUBLE-HOQUET* (Guillaume de Machaut) (1943)
Arranged for trumpet, horn and trombone

First performance: London, St Peter's Church (Eaton Square) 15
August 1943.
Malcolm Arnold (trumpet), Dennis Brain (horn) and George
Maxted (trombone)
Unpublished

W318.   *MOTET-MARIE ASSUMPTIO (*Anon. 13th century) (1943)
        Arranged for horn, trumpet and trombone

        First performance: London, St Peter's Church (Eaton Square), 15
            August 1943.
            Malcolm Arnold (trumpet), Dennis Brain (horn) and George
            Maxted (trombone)
        Unpublished

W319.   *ON THE BROW OF RICHMOND HILL* (Henry Purcell): 1959
        Song arranged for contralto and string orchestra
        Text by Tom Durfey

        Written for Pamela Bowden
        First performance: Richmond (Surrey), Community Centre Hall, 26
            March 1959.
            Pamela Bowden (contralto) and the Richmond Community Centre
            String Orchestra, conducted by Malcolm Arnold
        Unpublished

W320.   *ONLY A LITTLE BOX OF SOLDIERS* (1948)
        Music-hall song arranged for voice and piano
        Text by Fred Leigh

        First performance: Unable to trace
        Unpublished

W321.   *TANGO IN D* (Isaac Albeniz - Espana (Opus165 no.2)) (1953)
        Arranged for orchestra

        2.2.2.2/4.2.3.0/timpani percussion harp/strings

        First performance: unable to trace
        Unpublished

W322.   *THOMAS MERRITT - ANTHEMS AND CAROLS* (1968)

        1.   Carol: "Awake with joy, Salute the morn"
            arr. Mixed chorus, two brass bands and orchestra

            2+1.2.2.2/4.3.3.1/timpani percussion (3) harp/strings

        2.   Carol: "Send out the light"

<u>arr</u>. Mixed chorus and brass band

3. Anthem: "The Eyes of all wait for Thee"
   <u>arr</u>. Mixed chorus, harp and strings

4. Anthem: "Awake up my Glory"
   <u>arr</u>. Mixed chorus and orchestra

   2+1.2.2.2/4.3.3.1/timpani percussion (3)/strings

First performance: Truro, Cathedral Church, 16 March 1968.
    Mixed chorus, bands and Cornwall Symphony Orchestra conducted
    by Malcolm Arnold
Unpublished

W323. *THOMAS MERRITT: CORONATION MARCH* (1967)
    Arranged for brass band

    First performance: Truro, Cathedral Church, 16 March 1968.
        St Dennis Silver Band and St Agnes Silver Band, conducted by
        Malcolm Arnold
    Publication: Henrees Music, 1968

W324. *WE THREE KINGS OF ORIENT ARE* (1962)
    March arranged for piano and orchestra

    First performance: unable to trace
    Publication: Henrees Music, 1962

W325. *WILLIAM WALTON: SONATA FOR STRING ORCHESTRA* (1971)
    Arrangement of 2nd String Quartet (1947): 4th movement (Allegro
    molto) arranged by Malcolm Arnold for strings

    6.4.4.4.3 (strings)

    First performance: Perth Festival (Australia), 2 March 1972.
        Academy of St Martin-in-the-Fields, conducted by Neville Marriner
    Publication: Oxford University Press, 1973

Addendum

The following manuscripts have been recently re-discovered:

W326.   *THEME AND THREE VARIATIONS* (1937)
The manuscript (dated 20/1/1937) does not specify which instruments are to be used.

Andante Cantabile
Fugato: Andante Nobilmente
Bourèe: Allegro Vivace
Marcia Funebrè: Largo

W327.   *TWO SKETCHES FOR OBOE AND PIANO* (1941)

1.   Andante con moto
2.   Allegro vivace

The manuscript is dated 28 August 1941

DISCOGRAPHY

This select discography lists recently released recordings of Sir Malcolm Arnolds's music, all commercially produced on compact disc. The "see" references (e.g., SEE: B133) identify citations in the "Bibliography" section of this volume.

D1.   *ALLEGRO IN E MINOR* (W82)

         Benjamin Frith (piano)
         Koch International Classics 3 7162-2
         SEE: B141, B263

D2.   *BECKUS THE DANDIPRATT* (Opus 5) (W12)

         London Philharmonic Orchestra/Malcolm Arnold
         Reference Recordings RR 48 CD
         SEE:B144, B191

D3.   *THE BRIDGE ON THE RIVER KWAI:* Suite (W172)

         London Symphony Orchestra/Richard Hickox
         Chandos CHAN 9100
         SEE: B188

D4.   *CARNIVAL OF ANIMALS* (Opus 72) (W13)

         Royal Philharmonic Orchestra/Vernon Handley
         Conifer CDCF 240
         SEE: B97, B146, B261

D5.   *CHILDREN'S SUITE* (Opus 16) (W83)

Benjamin Frith (piano)
Koch International Classics 3 7162-2
SEE: B141, B263

D6.   *COMMONWEALTH CHRISTMAS OVERTURE* (Opus 64) (W14)

London Philharmonic Orchestra/Malcolm Arnold
Reference Recordings RR 48 CD
SEE: B144, B191

D7.   *CONCERTINO FOR OBOE AND STRINGS* (Opus 28A) (W126)

Nicholas Daniel (oboe)/Bournemouth Symphony Orchestra/Vernon
Handley
Conifer Classics 75605 51273-2
SEE: B200

D8.   *CONCERTO NO.1 for Clarinet and Orchestra* (Opus 20) (W15)

Emma Johnson (clarinet)/English Chamber Orchestra/Ivor Bolton
ASV CD DCA 922
SEE: B142, B184

Thea King (clarinet)/English Chamber Orchestra/Barry Wordsworth
Hyperion CDA 66634
SEE: B196

D9.   *CONCERTO NO.2 for Clarinet and Orchestra* (Opus 115) (W16)

Michael Collins (clarinet)/ London Musici/Mark Stephenson
Conifer CDCF 228
SEE: B192

Emma Johnson (clarinet)/English Chamber Orchestra/Ivor Bolton
ASV CD DCA 922
SEE: B142, B184

Thea King (clarinet)/English Chamber Orchestra/Barry Wordsworth
Hyperion CDA 66634
SEE: B196

D10.   *CONCERTO NO.2 for Flute and Chamber Orchestra* (Opus 111)
        (W18)

Karen Jones (flute)/ London Musici/Mark Stephenson
Conifer CDCF 228
SEE: B192

D11.   *CONCERTO for Guitar and Chamber Orchestra* (Opus 67) (W19)

Julian Bream (guitar)/City of Birmingham Symphony Orchestra/Simon
Rattle
EMI CDC7 54661-2
SEE: B155

Julian Bream (guitar)/Melos Ensemble
RCA 09026 61598-2
SEE : B272

Eduardo Fernandez (guitar)/English Chamber Orchestra/Barry
Wordsworth
Decca 430 233-2DH
SEE: B154

D12.   *CONCERTO NO.1 for Horn and Orchestra* (Opus 11) (W21)

Richard Watkins (horn)/London Musici/Mark Stephenson
Conifer CDCF 228
SEE: B192

D13.   *CONCERTO NO.2 for Horn and Orchestra* (Opus 58) (W22)

Alan Civil (horn)/English Chamber Orchestra/Malcolm Arnold
BBC Radio Classics 1565691817-2
SEE: B185

D14.   *CONCERTO for Piano Duet and Strings* (Opus 32) (W25)

David Nettle and Richard Markham (pianos)/London Musici/Mark
Stephenson
Conifer CDCF 228
SEE: B192

D15.   *CONCERTO for Recorder and Orchestra* (Opus 133) (W26)

Michala Petri (recorder)/English Chamber Orchestra/Okko Kamu
RCA Victor 09026 62543 2

D16.   *CONCERTO for Twenty Eight Players* (Opus 105) (W28)

City of London Sinfonia/Richard Hickox
Chandos CHAN 9509

London Musici/Mark Stephenson
Conifer CDCF 211
SEE: B190

D17.   *CONCERTO for Two Pianos (3 Hands) and Orchestra* (Opus 104)
(W29)

David Nettle and Richard Markham (pianos)/Royal Philharmonic
Orchestra/Vernon Handley
Conifer CDCF 240
SEE: B97, B146, B261

Cyril Smith and Phyllis Sellick (pianos)/BBC Symphony
Orchestra/Malcolm Arnold
BBC Radio Classics 1565691817-2
SEE: B185

D18.   *CONCERTO for Two Violins and String Orchestra* (Opus 77) (W30)

Igor Gruppman and Vesna Gruppman (violins)/San Diego Chamber
Orchestra/Donald Barra
Koch International Classics 37134-2
SEE: B189

Alan Loveday and Frances Mason (violins)/London Philharmonic
Orchestra/Malcolm Arnold
BBC Radio Classics 1565691817-2
SEE: B185

D19.   *CONCERTO for Viola and Chamber Orchestra* (Opus 105) (W31)

Roger Best (viola)/Northern Sinfonia/Malcolm Arnold
BBC Radio Classics 1565691817-2
SEE: B185

Rivka Golani (viola)/London Musici/Mark Stephenson
Conifer CDCF 211
SEE: B190

D20.   *DAY DREAMS* (W85)

Benjamin Frith (piano)
Koch International Classics 3 7162-2
SEE: B141, B263

D21.   *DIVERTIMENTO FOR FLUTE, OBOE AND CLARINET* (Opus 37)
(W86)

Jaime Martin (flute), Jonathan Kelly (oboe), Emma Johnson (clarinet)
ASV CD DCA 922
SEE: B142, B184

D22.   *EIGHT CHILDREN'S PIECES* (Opus 36) (W90)

Benjamin Frith (piano)
Koch International Classics 3 7162-2
SEE: B141, B263

D23.   *ENGLISH DANCES [Set 1]* (Opus 27) (W34)

Dallas Wind Symphony/Jerry Junkin
Reference Recordings RR66CD
SEE: B140

Grimethorpe Colliery Band/Elgar Howarth
Conifer CDCF 222
SEE: B258

London Philharmonic Orchestra/Malcolm Arnold
Lyrita/Conifer SRCD 201
SEE: B47, B187

Queensland Symphony Orchestra/Andrew Penny
Naxos 8.553526
SEE: B257

D24.   *ENGLISH DANCES [Set 2]* (Opus 33) (W35)

Grimethorpe Colliery Band/Elgar Howarth
Conifer CDCF 222
SEE: B258

London Philharmonic Orchestra/Malcolm Arnold
Lyrita/Conifer SRCD 201
SEE: B47, B187

Queensland Symphony Orchestra/Andrew Penny
Naxos 8.553526
SEE: B257

D25.   *FANFARE FOR LOUIS* (W295)

Dallas Wind Symphony/Jerry Junkin
Reference Recordings RR66CD
SEE: B140

D26.   *THE FAIR FIELD* (Opus 110) (W36)

BBC Symphony Orchestra/Malcolm Arnold
BBC Radio Classics 1565691817-2
SEE: B185

London Philharmonic Orchestra/Malcolm Arnold
Reference Recordings RR 48 CD
SEE: B144, B191

D27.   *FANTASY FOR BRASS BAND* (Opus 114a) (W298)

Grimethorpe Colliery Band/Elgar Howarth
Conifer CDCF 222
SEE: B258

D28.   *FANTASY FOR CELLO* (Opus 130) (W92)

Marcy Chanteaux (cello)
Koch International Classics 3 7266-2
SEE: B2

D29.   *FANTASY FOR CLARINET* (Opus 87) (W93)

Emma Johnson (clarinet)
ASV CD DCA 922
SEE: B142, B184

D30.   *FANTASY FOR HARP* (Opus 117) (W96)

Osian Ellis (harp)
BBC Radio Classics 1565691817-2
SEE: B185

D31.   *FANTASY FOR OBOE* (Opus 90) (W98)

Nicholas Daniel (oboe)
Conifer Classics 75605 51273-2
SEE: B200

D32.   *FANTASY ON A THEME OF JOHN FIELD* (Opus 116) (W38)

John Lill (piano)/Royal Philharmonic Orchestra/Vernon Handley
Conifer CDCF 224
SEE: B260

D33.   *FIVE WILLIAM BLAKE SONGS* (Opus 66) (W152)

Pamela Bowden (contralto)/BBC Northern Orchestra/Malcolm Arnold
BBC Radio Classics 1565691817-2
SEE: B185

D34.   *FIVE PIECES FOR VIOLIN AND PIANO* (Opus 84) (W104)

Emmanuelle Boisvert (violin)
Pauline Martin (piano)
Koch International Classics 3 7266-2
SEE: B2

D35.   *FOUR CORNISH DANCES* (Opus 91) (W41)

Grimethorpe Colliery Band/Elgar Howarth
Conifer CDCF 222
SEE: B258

London Philharmonic Orchestra/Malcolm Arnold
BBC Radio Classics 1565691817-2
SEE: B185

London Philharmonic Orchestra/Malcolm Arnold
Lyrita/Conifer SRCD 201
SEE: B47, B187

Queensland Symphony Orchestra/Andrew Penny
Naxos 8.553526
SEE: B257

D36.   *FOUR IRISH DANCES* (Opus 126) (W42)

London Philharmonic Orchestra/Malcolm Arnold
Lyrita/Conifer SRCD 201
SEE: B47, B187

Queensland Symphony Orchestra/Andrew Penny
Naxos 8.553526
SEE: B257

D37.   *FOUR SCOTTISH DANCES* (Opus 59) (W43)

Dallas Wind Symphony/Jerry Junkin
Reference Recordings RR66CD
SEE: B140

Grimethorpe Colliery Band/Elgar Howarth
Conifer CDCF 222
SEE: B258

London Philharmonic Orchestra/Malcolm Arnold
Lyrita/Conifer SRCD 201
SEE: B47, B187

Queensland Symphony Orchestra/Andrew Penny
Naxos 8.553526
SEE: B257

Scots Guards Band/Price
Bandleader BNA 5038
SEE: B102

D38.   *FOUR WELSH DANCES* (Opus 138) (W44)

Queensland Symphony Orchestra/Andrew Penny
Naxos 8.553526
SEE: B257

D39.   *A GRAND GRAND OVERTURE (Opus 57) (W46)*

Royal Philharmonic Orchestra/Vernon Handley
Conifer CDCF 240
SEE: B97, B146, B261

D40.   *HRH THE DUKE OF CAMBRIDGE* (Opus 60) (W301)

Dallas Wind Symphony/Jerry Junkin
Reference Recordings RR66CD
SEE: B140

D41.   *HOBSON'S CHOICE*: Suite (W200)

London Symphony Orchestra/Richard Hickox
Chandos CHAN 9100
SEE: B188

HOBSON'S CHOICE: (arr. Hogan)

St. Clair Trio
Koch International Classic 3 7266-2
SEE: B2

D42.   *THE HOLLY AND THE IVY* : Fantasy on Christmas Carols (W201)
consisting of:
      The Holly and the Ivy (W201)
      Arrangements of Christmas Carols (W316)
      Commonwealth Christmas Overture (W14)

St. Paul's Cathedral Choir/Royal Philharmonic Orchestra/John Scott
RPO Records RPO 7021

D43.   *HOMAGE TO THE QUEEN* (Opus 42) (W6)

Philharmonia Orchestra/Robert Irving
EMI CDM 5 66120 2
SEE: B156

HOMAGE TO THE QUEEN (Opus 42) arr. for piano (W6)

Pauline Martin (piano)
Koch International Classics 3 7266-2
SEE: B2

D44.   *THE INN OF THE SIXTH HAPPINESS*: Suite (W206)

London Symphony Orchestra/Richard Hickox
Chandos CHAN 9100
SEE: B188

D45.   *LARCH TREES* (Opus 3) (W47)

London Musici/Mark Stephenson
Conifer CDCF 211
SEE: B190

D46.   *LITTLE SUITE [NO.1] for Brass Band* (Opus 80) (W304)

Dallas Wind Symphony/Jerry Junkin
Reference Recordings RR66CD
SEE: B140

Grimethorpe Colliery Band/Elgar Howarth
Conifer CDCF 222

D47.   *LITTLE SUITE [NO.2] for Brass Band* (Opus 93) (W305)

Dallas Wind Symphony/Jerry Junkin
Reference Recordings RR66CD
SEE: B140

Grimethorpe Colliery Band/Elgar Howarth
Conifer CDCF222

D48.   *LITTLE SUITE [NO.1] for Orchestra* (Opus 53) (W78)

City of London Sinfonia/Richard Hickox
Chandos CHAN 9509

D49.   *LITTLE SUITE [NO.2] for Orchestra* (Opus 78) (W49)

City of London Sinfonia/Richard Hickox
Chandos CHAN 9509

D50.   *A MANX SUITE* (Opus 142) (W50)

City of London Sinfonia/Richard Hickox

Chandos CHAN 9509

D51. *MARCH: OVERSEAS* (Opus 70) (W307)

Dallas Wind Symphony/Jerry Junkin
Reference Recordings RR66CD
SEE: B140

D52. *THE PADSTOW LIFEBOAT* (Opus 94) (W308)

Dallas Wind Symphony/Jerry Junkin
Reference Recordings RR66CD
SEE: B140

Grimethorpe Colliery Band/Malcolm Arnold
Conifer CDCF 222
SEE: B258

D53. *PETERLOO* (Opus 97) (W51)

BBC Symphony Orchestra/Malcolm Arnold
BBC Radio Classics 1565691817-2
SEE: B185

City of Birmingham Symphony Orchestra/Malcolm Arnold
EMI Studio CDM7 63368-2
SEE: B51, B253

D54. *POPULAR BIRTHDAY* (1972) (W53)

London Philharmonic Orchestra/Jan Latham-König
Chandos CHAN 9148
SEE: B183

D55. *PRELUDE* (W111)

Benjamin Frith (piano)
Koch International Classics 3 7162-2
SEE: B141, B263

D56. *QUARTET [NO.1] for Strings* (Opus 23) (W113)

McCapra Quartet

Chandos CHAN 9112
SEE: B50, B143, B199, B219

D57.   *QUARTET [NO.2] for Strings* (Opus 118) (W114)

McCapra Quartet
Chandos CHAN 9112
SEE: B50, B143, B199, B219

D58.   *SARABANDE AND POLKA: SOLITAIRE* (W8)

London Philharmonic Orchestra/Malcolm Arnold
Lyrita/Conifer SRCD 201
SEE: B47, B187

D59.   *SERENADE FOR SMALL ORCHESTRA* (Opus 26) (W57)

London Musici/Mark Stephenson
Conifer CDCF 211
SEE: B190

San Diego Chamber Orchestra/Donald Barra
Koch International Classics 37134-2
SEE: B189

D60.   *SERENADE IN G* (W117)

Benjamin Frith (piano)
Koch International Classics 3 7162-2
SEE: B141, B263

D61.   *SINFONIETTA NO.1* (Opus 48) (W59)

English Chamber Orchestra/Malcolm Arnold
BBC Radio Classics 1565691817-2
SEE: B185

San Diego Chamber Orchestra/Donald Barra
Koch International Classics 37134-2
SEE: B189

D62.   *SINFONIETTA [NO.2]* (Opus 65) (W60)

San Diego Chamber Orchestra/Donald Barra
Koch International Classics 37134-2
SEE: B189

D63.   *THE SMOKE* (Opus 21) (W62)

London Philharmonic Orchestra/Malcolm Arnold
Reference Recordings RR 48 CD
SEE: B144, B191

D64.   *SONATA FOR PIANO* (W120)

Benjamin Frith (piano)
Koch International Classics 3 7162-2
SEE: B141, B263

D65.   *SONATINA FOR CLARINET AND PIANO* (Opus 29) (W124)

Emma Johnson (clarinet) and Malcolm Martineau (piano)
ASV CD DCA 922
SEE: B142, B184

D66.   *SONG OF SIMEON* (Opus 69) (W147)

Soloists/English Chamber Orchestra/Malcolm Arnold
BBC Radio Classics 1565691817-2
SEE: B185

D67.   *THE SOUND BARRIER* (Opus 38) (W247)

London Symphony Orchestra/Richard Hickox
Chandos CHAN 9100
SEE: B188

D68.   *A SUSSEX OVERTURE* (Opus 31) (W64)

London Philharmonic Orchestra/Malcolm Arnold
Reference Recordings RR 48 CD
SEE: B144, B191

D69.   *SWEENEY TODD:* Suite (Opus 68a) (W9)

Royal Philharmonic Orchestra/Vernon Handley

Conifer CDCF 224
SEE: B260

D70.   *SYMPHONY NO. 1* (Opus 22) (W67)

London Symphony Orchestra/Richard Hickox
Chandos CHAN 9335
SEE: B264

National Symphony Orchestra of Ireland/Andrew Penny
Naxos 8.553406
SEE: B137, B266, B337

Royal Philharmonic Orchestra/Vernon Handley
Conifer Classics 75605 51257-2
SEE: B96, B267

D71.   *SYMPHONY NO.2* (Opus 40) (W68)

Bournemouth Symphony Orchestra/Charles Groves
EMI Studio CDM7 63368-2
SEE: B51, B253

London Symphony Orchestra/Richard Hickox
Chandos CHAN 9335
SEE: B264

National Symphony Orchestra of Ireland/Andrew Penny
Naxos 8.553406
SEE: B137, B266, B337

Royal Philharmonic Orchestra/Vernon Handley
Conifer CDCF 240
SEE: B97, B146, B261

D72.   *SYMPHONY NO.3* (Opus 63) (W69)

London Symphony Orchestra/Richard Hickox
Chandos CHAN 9290
SEE: B145, B270

Royal Liverpool Philharmonic Orchestra/Vernon Handley
Conifer Classics 75605 51258-2

SEE: B262

D73.   *SYMPHONY NO.4* (Opus 71) (W70)

London Philharmonic Orchestra/Malcolm Arnold
Lyrita/Conifer SRCD200
SEE: B6, B269

London Symphony Orchestra/Richard Hickox
Chandos CHAN 9290
SEE: B145, B270

Royal Liverpool Philharmonic Orchestra/Vernon Handley
Conifer Classics 75605 51258-2
SEE: B262

D74.   *SYMPHONY NO.5* (Opus 74) (W71)

City of Birmingham Symphony Orchestra/Malcolm Arnold
EMI Studio CDM7 63368-2
SEE: B51, B253

London Symphony Orchestra/Richard Hickox
Chandos CHAN 9385
SEE: B138, B265

Royal Philharmonic Orchestra/Vernon Handley
Conifer Classics 75605 51257-2
SEE: B96, B267

D75.   *SYMPHONY NO.6* (Opus 95) (W72)

London Symphony Orchestra/Richard Hickox
Chandos CHAN 9385
SEE: B138, B265

Royal Philharmonic Orchestra/Vernon Handley
Conifer CDCF 224
SEE: B260

D76.   *SYMPHONY NO.7* (Opus 113) (W73)

Royal Philharmonic Orchestra/Vernon Handley

Conifer CDCF 177
SEE: B6, B274

D77. *SYMPHONY NO.8* (Opus 124) (W74)

Royal Philharmonic Orchestra/Vernon Handley
Conifer CDCF 177
SEE: B6, B274

D78. *SYMPHONY NO.9* (Opus 128) W75

Bournemouth Symphony Orchestra/Vernon Handley
Conifer Classics 75605 51273-2
SEE: B200

National Symphony Orchestra of Ireland/Andrew Penny
Naxos 8.553540
SEE:B139, B247, B271

D79. *TAM O'SHANTER* (Opus 51) (W76)

Dallas Wind Symphony/Jerry Junkin
Reference Recordings RR66CD
SEE: B140

Royal Philharmonic Orchestra/Vernon Handley
Conifer CDCF 224
SEE: B260

Scots Guards Band/Price
Bandleader BNA 5038
SEE: B102

D80. *THREE FANTASIES* (Opus 129) (W129)

Benjamin Frith (piano)
Koch International Classics 3 7162-2
SEE: B141, B263

D81. *THREE PIANO PIECES* (W130)

Benjamin Frith (piano)
Koch International Classics 3 7162-2

SEE: B141, B263

D82.   *THREE PIANO PIECES* (W131)

Benjamin Frith (piano)
Koch International Classics 3 7162-2
SEE: B141, B263

D83.   *THREE SHANTIES FOR WIND QUINTET* (Opus 4) (W132)

Claire Briggs (horn)/Susanna Cohen (bassoon)/Emma Johnson
(clarinet)/Jonathan Kelly (oboe)/Jaime Martin (flute)
ASV CD DCA 922
SEE: B142, B184

D84.   *TRIO FOR VIOLIN, CELLO AND PIANO* (Opus 54) (W135)

St. Clair Trio
Koch International Classics 3 7622-2
SEE: B2

D85.   *TWO BAGATELLES* (Opus 18) (W136)

Benjamin Frith (piano)
Koch International Classics 3 7162-2
SEE: B141, B263

D86.   *TWO PIANO PIECES* (W137)

Benjamin Frith (piano)
Koch International Classics 3 7162-2
SEE: B141, B263

D87.   *VARIATIONS FOR ORCHESTRA ON A THEME OF RUTH GIPPS*
(Opus 122) (W81)

City of London Sinfonia/Richard Hickox
Chandos CHAN 9509

D88.   *VARIATIONS ON AN UKRAINIAN FOLKSONG* (Opus 9) (W138)

Benjamin Frith (piano)
Koch International Classics 3 7162-2

SEE: B141, B263

D89.   *WATER MUSIC* (Opus 82) (W315)

Dallas Wind Symphony/Jerry Junkin
Reference Recordings RR66CD
SEE: B140

D90.   *WHISTLE DOWN THE WIND*: Suite (W267)

London Symphony Orchestra/Richard Hickox
Chandos CHAN 9100
SEE: B188

D91.   *YOU KNOW WHAT SAILORS ARE - SCHERZETTO* (W273)

English Chamber Orchestra/Barry Wordsworth
Hyperion CDA66634
SEE: B196

BIBLIOGRAPHY

The "see" references refer to individual works and performances of these works as described in the "Works and Performances" section (e.g., SEE: W133) and in the "Discography" section (e.g., SEE: D33).

B1.   A., H.F. "Malcolm Arnold - Bright Young Man of British Music."
        Gloucestershire Echo, 18 July 1957, p.5.

        An early appreciation, prompted by the first performance of Arnold's *2nd Concerto for Horn and Strings*. SEE: W22

B2.   Achenbach, A. [Arnold: Recordings]
        Gramophone, 74 (November 1996), p.104.

        A review of the Koch International Classics recording 37266-2. SEE: D28, D34, D41, D43, D84

B3.   Adeney, R. "Tribute."
        In 65th birthday concert programme (1986).

        A birthday tribute.

B4.   Adler, L. "Tribute."
        In 65th birthday concert programme (1986).

        A birthday tribute.

B5.   Anderson, M. "Book Review."
        Tempo No.171 (December 1989), p.42.

        A review of Hugo Cole's introduction to the music of Malcolm Arnold.

B6.   Anderson, M. "Record Reviews."
        Tempo, no. 178 (September 1991), pp.51-52.

        Views on Lyrita SRCD 200 (Symphony No. 4), and Conifer
        CDCF 177 (Symphonies Nos 7 and 8). SEE: D73, D76, D77

B7.   Andry, P. "Tribute."
        In 65th birthday concert programme (1986).

        A birthday tribute.

B8.   Angles, R. "Arnold conducts Arnold."
        Music and Musicians, 13 (March 1965), p.38.

        An account of a concert at the Fairfield Hall, Croydon, when
        Arnold conducted the premiere of his *Sinfonietta No. 3* SEE:
        W61

B9.   Anon. "Albany Symphony: Malcolm Arnold premiere."
        HI FI/Musical America, 29 (September 1979), p.MA26.

        Details about the *8th Symphony*. SEE: W74

B10.   Anon. [Arnold's Knighthood]
        Gramophone, 10 (April 1993), p.12.

        Brief details and a photograph of the composer at Buckingham
        Palace.

B11.   Anon. "B.R.'s Hallé."
        Music and Musicians, 32 (February 1984), p.3.

        A mention of Arnold's *Railway Fanfare*. SEE: W311

B12.   Anon. "Barbirolli leads Arnold overture."
        Musical America, 79 (15 January 1959), p.18.

        A review of an American concert which included *Tam
        O'Shanter*. SEE: W76

B13.   Anon. "Birthday congratulations."
        Classical Guitar, 10 (October 1991), p.5.

70th birthday greetings to the composer.

B14.   Anon. "Book reviews."
       Royal College of Music Magazine." 87, no.1 (1990).
       pp.60-61.

       A review of Hugo Cole's introduction to Arnold's music.

B15.   Anon. [Concerto for Harmonica, Opus 46]
       London Music, 9 (November 1954), p.42.

       Mention of the printed miniature score, published by
       Patersons. SEE: W20

B16.   Anon. "Editorial notes."
       Strad, 58 (January 1947), pp. 259-260.

       Remarks about Arnold's first *Concerto for Horn and Orchestra.*
       SEE: W21

B17.   Anon. "Editorial notes."
       Strad, 63 (September 1952), p.141.

       Mention of the first performance of the Second Set of *English
       Dances.* SEE: W35

B18.   Anon. "Editorial notes."
       Strad, 65 (July 1954), p.69.

       Mention of Arnold's *2nd Symphony.* SEE: W68

B19.   Anon. "Editorial notes."
       Strad, 70 (July 1959), pp.83+.

       Mention of the composer.

B20.   Anon. "Editorial notes."
       Strad, 71 (April 1961), p.461.

       Mention of Arnold's *4th Symphony.* SEE: W70

B21.   Anon. "Exeter degree for Cornish composer."
       The Western Morning News, 3 July 1970, p.3.

An account of the ceremony at Exeter University when Arnold received an honorary degree of Doctor of Music.

B22.   Anon. [Fantasy for recorder and string quartet.]
          American Recorder, 32, no.2 (1991), p.6.

          Mention of Opus 140. SEE: W100

B23.   Anon. "Film music and beyond."
          Music Review, 17 (November 1956), pp.336-337.

          Reflections on film music, with mention of Arnold's score for A *Hill in Korea* . SEE: W199

B24.   Anon. "Film music and beyond."
          Music Review, 19 (May 1958), pp.150-151.

          Mention of Arnold's score for *Bridge on the River Kwai*. SEE: W172

B25.   Anon. "First performances."
          Music Review, 13 (February 1952), pp. 43-44.

          Details about the first performances of the *First String Quartet* and the *First Symphony*. SEE: W 67, W113

B26.   Anon. [Flourish for a battle]
          Music and Musicians, 38 (April 1990), p.4.

          A brief mention of Arnold's *Flourish for a Battle*. SEE: W299

B27.   Anon. "Grand Concerto Gastronomique."
          Musica, 16, no.2 (1962), p.93.

          A mention (in German) of Arnold's *Grand Concerto Gastronomique*. SEE: W45

B28.   Anon. "Hallé concerto 1961-62."
          Music Review, 23, no.3 (1962), pp.249-250.

          Mention of the premiere of Arnold's *5th Symphony* by the Hallé Orchestra. SEE: W71

B29.   Anon. "High Notes."
        Musical Opinion, 116 (February 1993), p.42.

        Details of the New Year's Honours List and Arnolds's
        Knighthood.

B30.   Anon. "Like blowing a gaspipe!"
        Northampton Independent, 5 November 1937, p.3.

        An account of the 16-year-old Arnold playing the trumpet in
        Bach's 2nd Brandenburg Concerto.

B31.   Anon. "Malcolm Arnold-Anti-Theorist."
        The Times, 11 May 1959, p.3.

        Arnold's views on being a composer.

B32.   Anon. "Malcolm Arnold at 65."
        The British Bandsman, 25 October 1986, p.5.

        An interview about Arnold's involvement with brass bands.

B33.   Anon. "Malcolm Arnold, creator of *Beckus*."
        Winter Gardens Society Magazine, Winter 1951, pp.7-8

        Views on Arnold's career

B34.   Anon. "Malcolm Arnold's Cello Concerto."
        Music and Musicians, 37 (March 1989), p.2.

        An announcement about the premiere of Arnold's *Cello
        Concerto*. SEE: W58

B35.   Anon. "Malcolm was 'walcolm'."
        Music (SMA), 3, no.2 (1969), p.46.

        Description of a concert organised by the Schools Musical
        Association.

B36.   Anon. "More from Kenneth Jones."
        Strad, 73 (May 1962), p.35.

        Mention of the concert, conducted by Kenneth Jones, when

Arnold's *Divertimento No.2* was first performed in London. SEE: W33

B37.   Anon. "Music-Malcolm Arnold's 3rd Symphony."
Truth, 13 December 1957, p.1414.

A review of the *Third Symphony*. SEE: W69

B38.   Anon. "Music in honour of lifeboat men."
Cornish Guardian, 27 June 1968, p.1.

Details about the first performance in Cornwall of Arnold's March, *The Padstow Lifeboat*. SEE: W308

B39.   Anon. "New Malcolm Arnold work for Julian Lloyd Webber."
Music and Musicians, 35 (November 1987), p.7.

Details about the *Fantasy for Cello*. SEE: W92

B40.   Anon. [New Year Honours]
The Daily Telegraph, 31 December 1992, p.11.

The official announcement about the composer's knighthood.

B41.   Anon. "New York."
Music Journal, 35 (February 1977), pp.34-35.

A description of *Philharmonic Concerto* and its first performance. SEE: W52

B42.   Anon. "News in brief."
Royal College of Music Magazine, 89, no.2 (1992), p.36.

Mention of *Symphony No.9*. SEE: W75

B43.   Anon. "Nostalgia?"
Musical Opinion, 93 (October 1969), pp.5-6.

Views on the proposed *Fantasy for Audience and Orchestra*. SEE: W37

B44.   Anon. "Oscar winner who believes in simplicity."
Bristol Evening Post, 28 March 1967, p.5.

A brief interview with the composer.

B45.   Anon. "Premieres."
        Symphony News, 30, no.3 (1979), pp.80+.

        Details about the premiere in Albany, New York, of Arnold's *8th Symphony*. SEE: W74

B46.   Anon. "The Promenade Concerts."
        Strad, 80 (October 1969), p.282.

        A survey of the 1969 season of Promenade Concerts, with mention of Arnold's *Concerto of 2 pianos (3 hands) and Orchestra*. SEE: W

B47.   Anon. "Record Reviews."
        Stereo Review, 56 (July 1991), p.79.

        A review of Lyrita/Conifer SRCD 201. See: D23, D24, D35, D36, D37, D58

B48.   Anon. "Recordings in review."
        Musical America, 110, No.1 (1990), pp.55-56.

        A review of recordings of Arnold's chamber music.

B49.   Anon. "Recordings in review."
        Musical America, 110, No.7 (1990), p.68.

        Notes on recordings of Arnold's chamber music.

B50.   Anon. "Review: CDs - Arnold: String Quartet Nos 1 and 2 (The McCapra Quartet)."
        Strad, 104 (August 1993), p.104.

        A review of the Chandos recording. SEE: D56, D57

B51.   Anon. "Reviews - recordings."
        Royal College of Music Magazine, 87, no.3 (1990), pp.57-58.

        A review of EMI Studio CDM 7 63368-2. SEE: D53, D71, D74

B52.   Anon. "Reviews of new music."

Musical Opinion, 74 (April 1951), p.345.

A review of the miniature score of the *English Dances* (Sct 1). SEE:W34

B53.   Anon.   "Reviews of new music."
         Musical Opinion, 75 (November 1951), p.97.

         Views on the published score of Arnold's *Sonatina for oboe and piano*. SEE: W126

B54.   Anon.   "Reviews of new music."
         Musical Opinion, 75 (December 1951), p.159.

         A review of the printed score of Arnold's *String Quartet No.1*. SEE: W113

B55.   Anon.   "Reviews of new music."
         Musical Opinion, 75 (July 1952), pp.605+607.

         Notes on the published score of Arnold's *Concerto for Clarinet and Strings*. SEE: W15

B56.   Anon.   "Reviews of new music."
         Musical Opinion, 75 (July 1952), p.605.

         Mention of the published score of Arnold's *Divertimento for flute, oboe and clarinet*. See: W86

B57.   Anon.   "Reviews of new music."
         Musical Opinion 75 (July 1952), p.605.

         Views on *Symphony No.1* and its printed score. SEE: W67

B58.   Anon.   "Reviews of new music."
         Musical Opinion, 76 (July 1953), p.611.

         A review of the printed score of Arnold's *2nd Symphony*. SEE: W68

B59.   Anon. [Reviews of new music.]
         Music Teacher, 33 (April 1954), p.212.

Mention of *Symphony No. 2*. SEE: W68

B60.   Anon. "Reviews of new music."
       Musical Opinion, 77 (May 1954), pp.479+481.

       Notes on the printed score of Arnold's *Concerto for flute and strings*. SEE: W17

B61.   Anon. [Reviews of new music.]
       Music Review, 15 (May 1954). pp.147-148.

       Mention of the score of Arnold's *Divertimento for flute, oboe and clarinet*. SEE: W86

B62.   Anon. "Reviews of new music."
       Musical Opinion, 77 (September 1954), p.713.

       A review of the score of Arnold's *Trio for flute, viola and bassoon*. SEE: W134

B63.   Anon. [Reviews of new music.]
       Musical Opinion, 78 (August 1955), p.673.

       Views on the published miniature score of *Tam O'Shanter*. SEE: W76

B64.   Anon. [Reviews of new music.]
       Violins, 15 (November-December 1954), p.283.

       A reviews of the score of Arnold's *Concerto for flute and strings* SEE: W17

B65.   Anon. [Reviews of new music.]
       London Music, 10 (March 1955), p.35.

       A review of the published score of Arnold's *Sinfonietta No.1*, SEE: W59

B66.   Anon. [Reviews of new music.]
       Music Review, 16 (March 1955), pp.165-166.

       A review of the score of Arnold's *Concerto for flute and strings*. SEE: W17

B67.   Anon. [Reviews of new music.]
         Music Review, 16 (May 1955), pp.161-163.

         Details about the printed miniature score of Arnold's *Symphony No.2.* SEE: W68

B68.   Anon. [Reviews of new music.]
         Music Review, 16 (May 1955), pp.165-166.

         A review of the score of Arnold's *Sonatina for recorder and piano.* SEE: W127

B69.   Anon. [Reviews of new music.]
         Notes, 14 (June 1957), p.453.

         Mention of the printed score of Arnold's *Little Suite for Orchestra.* SEE: W78

B70.   Anon. [Reviews of new music.]
         Musical Opinion, 92 (July 1968), p.551.

         A review of the score of Arnold's *Four Cornish Dances.* SEE: W41

B71.   Anon. [Reviews of new music.]
         Notes, 45, no.1 (1988), pp.153-154.

         A description of the printed score of Arnold's *Concerto for Clarinet No.2.* SEE. W16

B72.   Anon. "Royal Liverpool Philharmonic Orchestra."
         London Music, 13 (January 1958), p.43.

         Details about the first performance of *Symphony No.3.* SEE: W69

B73.   Anon. "Spring Term 1983 programmes."
         Royal College of Music Magazine, 78, no.2 (1983), p.84.

         Details of Arnold's *Trumpet Concerto.* SEE: W27

B74.   Anon. "Stage and Screen: The Sound Barrier at the Plaza."
         Theatre, 2 August 1952, p.8.

A review of the film, *The Sound Barrier*. SEE: W247

B75.   Anon. "Symphony No.4 (Opus 71)."
        Music and Musicians, 9 (April 1961), p.36.

        A review of the printed score. SEE: W70

B76.   Anon. "Tam breaks record."
        Music and Musicians, 5 (April 1957), p.21.

        Details of the early performances of *Tam O'Shanter*. SEE: W76

B77.   Anon. "Tam O' Shanter Overture."
        Detroit Symphony Orchestra Program Notes, 3 March 1966,
        p.441+.

        An analysis of and commentary on the overture. SEE: W76

B78.   Anon. "Tam O' Shanter."
        Houston Symphony Orchestra Program Notes, 27 March 1967,
        pp.15-17.

        An analysis of the overture. SEE: W76

B79.   Anon. [Trio of flute, violin and bassoon.]
        London Music, 9 (November 1954), p.42.

        A review of the published score. SEE: W134

B80.   Anon. "West of the line."
        Music and Musicians, 17 (August 1969), p.41.

        Views of and news about Arnold.

B81.   Ariel. "All made in Northampton."
        Northampton Independent, 1 May 1953, p.6.

        A photograph and account of three composers born in
        Northampton: William Alwyn, Malcolm Arnold and Edmund
        Rubbra.

B82.   Arnold, M. "Don't shoot the pianist."
        The Guardian, 3 June 1971, p.10.

The composer's views on music critics.

B83.   Arnold, M. "Film Music."
         Recorded Sound, no.18 (April 1965), pp.328-334.

         The text of a lecture given by Arnold on writing film music.

B84.   Arnold, M. "Finding the Money."
         The Sunday Times Magazine, 2 November 1958, p.20.

         A discussion about the performance of new music.

B85.   Arnold, M. "I think of music in terms of sand."
         Music and Musicians, 4 (July 1956), p.9.

         An explanation by the composer of his method of working and
         writing music.

B86.   Arnold, M. "Language of Modern Music in Complete Chaos."
         Gloucestershire Echo, 24 March 1961, p.4.

         The composer's views on modern music.

B87.   Arnold, M. "My Early Life."
         Music and Musicians, 34 (October 1986), pp.8-9.

         An autobiographical reminiscence in which the composer looks
         back to the beginning of his career.

B88.   Arnold, M. [Music I enjoy.]
         The Listener, 86 (14 October 1971), p.518.

         A personal account of the composer's likes in music.

B89.   Arnold, M. "On the birth of a Dandipratt."
         Winter Gardens Society Magazine, Winter 1951, p.8.

         An explanation of Arnold's overture *Beckus the Dandipratt.*
         SEE: W12

B90.   Arnold, M. "Prof. Hans Knappertsbusch - letter to the Times."
         The Times, 4 November 1965, p.7.

An addition in the form of personal note, to a recent obituary.

B91.   Arnold, M and Gilliat, S. "St. Trinian's School Song."
       In Webb, K. "The St. Trinian's Story."
       Harmondsworth, Penguin Books, 1959, pp.48-49.

       The theme music for *The Belles of St. Trinian's* and theme song
       for *Blue Murder at St. Trinian's.* SEE: W169, W170

B92.   Arnold, W. "Malcolm Arnold's musical ancestry."
       Musical Events, 15 (November 1960), p.8.

       A brief account, by the composer's father, of Malcolm's musical
       ancestry.

B93.   Bach, E.S. "A performance project on selected works of five
       composers."
       D.M.A. dissertation, University of British Columbia (Canada),
       1991.

       A detailed discussion of music for unaccompanied trumpet
       composed after 1965. Chapter II is devoted to Arnold's *Fantasy
       for Trumpet.* SEE: W102

B94.   Baggs, G. "Malcolm Arnold at home."
       The Western Morning News, 17 October 1969, p.3.

       A detailed and useful interview with the composer.

B95.   Banfield, S. "Orchestral, choral."
       Musical Times, 127 (November 1986), p.628.

       A review of the score of Arnold's *Concerto for 28 players.*
       SEE: W28

B96.   Barfoot, T. "Arnold: Symphonies 1 and 5."
       BBC Music Magazine, 4 (August 1996), p.72.

       A review of the Conifer recording 75605 5125 7-2. SEE: D70,
       D74

B97.   Barfoot, T. "Orchestral."
       BBC Music Magazine, 3 (February 1995), p.72.

A review of Conifer CDCF 240. SEE: D4, D17, D39, D71

B98.   Barfoot, T. "Recording Report: Arnold on Naxos."
BBC Music Magazine, 4 (March 1996), p.54.

Details of and an introduction to the recording of a new cycle of
Arnold's symphonies.

B99.   Barnes, C. "Apeneck Sweeney."
The Spectator, 18 December 1959, p.910.

An appreciation of Arnold's ballet, *Sweeney Todd*. SEE: W9

B100.   Barnes, C. "Glory! Glory! Glory! From one man of brass to five others."
Daily Express, 16 May 1968, p.4.

An examination of the virtuosity of the New York Brass Quintet.

B101.   Bashford, R. "Brass and Military."
Gramophone, 66 (January 1989), p.1215.

A record review.

B102.   Bashford, R. "Brass and Military."
Gramophone, 68 (August 1990), pp.411-412.

A review of Bandleader BNA 5038. SEE: D37, D79

B103.   Bashford, R. "Brass and Military."
Gramophone, 68 (November 1990), pp. 1060+1065.

A record review.

B104.   Blanks, H. "Music in England in June 1954."
Canon, 8 (August 1954), p.26.

An account of first performances, including the first London
performance of Arnold's *2nd Symphony*. SEE: W68

B105.   Blyth, A. "Arnold: English Dances."
Gramophone, 68 (September 1990), p.598.

A record review.

B106.   Bowman, G. "War in the Air."
        London, Evans Brothers, 1956.

        Useful background information to the BBC television film series
        with music by Arnold. SEE: W291

B107.   Bowyen, D. "Unfair to Arnold - and to us!"
        Croydon Advertiser, 29 January 1965, p.7.

        Views on Arnold's recorded works.

B108.   Boyd, M.. "Cardiff, St. David's."
        Musical Times, 118 (May 1977), pp.413-414.

        Mention of Arnold's *Sonata for flute and piano* and its first
        performance. SEE: W119

B109.   Bradbury, E. "Divertimento."
        Programme note for the first London performance, BBC
        Promenade Concert, 10 August 1957. SEE: W33

B110.   Bray, T. "Reviews of Books."
        Music and Letters. 71,no.3 (1990), pp.443-444.

        Views on Hugo Cole's book on Arnold and his music.

B111.   Bream, J. "Tribute."
        In 65th birthday concert programme (1986).

        A birthday tribute.

B112.   Buckle, R. "Helpmann in a blaze."
        The Sunday Times, 31 March 1963, p.40.

        Views on the first performance of Arnold's ballet *Electra*.
        SEE:W5

B113.   Burges, P. "Malcolm Arnold's Fourth Symphony."
        Musical Events, 15 (December 1960), pp.10-11.

        Views on and reaction to Arnold's *Fourth Symphony*.
        SEE: W70

B114.   Burton-Page, P. "Arnold at 70."
         Musical Times, 132 (October 1991), pp.493-495.

         A survey of Arnold's life and music.

B115.   Burton-Page, P. "Arnold's Ninth."
         BBC Philharmonic Orchestra Friends Magazine, 33 (Winter
         1991-1992), pp.8-10.

         A description of the *Ninth Symphony*. SEE: W75

B116.   Burton-Page, P. "Malcolm Arnold and the String Quartet."
         Musical Times, 127 (October 1986), pp.551-554.

         A description of Arnold's string quartets of 1949 and 1975.
         SEE: W113, W114

B117.   Burton-Page, P. "Philharmonic Concerto."
         London, Methuen, 1994.

         The first authorised biography of the composer, written with the
         full co-operation of Sir Malcolm.

B118.   Burton-Page, P. "Six paradoxes in search of a composer."
         From Silents to Satellite, 10 (Autumn 1991), pp.22-24.

         Views on Arnold and his music.

B119.   C., M.. "Off the beaten music track."
         Daily Herald, 21 May 1947, p.3.

         A brief mention of an early performance of Arnold's *Wind
         Quintet*. SEE: W116

B120.   Carpenter, J. "The News Diary."
         The Evening News, 28 December 1955, p.4.

         An article looking forward to 1956 with a mention of Malcolm
         Arnold who is described as "our leading young composer."

B121.   Chanan, M. "Albert Hall."
         Music and Musicians, 18 (December 1969), p.57.

A review of a concert conducted by the composer.

B122.   Chapman. E. "Malcolm Arnold's opera."
         Musical Events, 17 (April 1962), p.12.

         Mention of Arnold's opera, *The Dancing Master*, first performed
         in Barnes, London, March 1962. SEE: W1

B123.   Chapman, E. "Opera at Morley College."
         Musical Events, 17 (February 1962), p.29.

         Mention of a performance of Arnold's one-act opera *The Open
         Window*. SEE: W3

B124.   Chissell, J. "R.C.M. Gala."
         The Times, 1 February 1983, p.8.

         An account of the concert at the Royal Albert Hall in London
         when Arnold's *Trumpet Concerto* was first performed. SEE:
         W27

B125.   Cohn, A. "Malcolm Arnold."
         In his "Twentieth-Century Music in Western Europe."
         Philadelphia, J.B. Lippincott, 1965, pp.3-7 and 358-359.

         A useful survey of Arnold's music.

B126.   Cole, H. "Arnold's Fantasies."
         Music and Musicians International, 36 (December 1987),
         pp.22-23.

         Useful background to Arnold's series of Fantasies for various
         solo instruments.

B127.   Cole, H. "Malcolm Arnold."
         In Grove's Dictionary of Music and Musicians, London,
         Macmillan, 1980; 6th edition, volume 1, pp.615-616.

         A useful summary of Arnold's life and music, together with a list
         of works.

B128.   Cole, H. "Malcolm Arnold: an appreciation."
         In Poulton, A. "The Music of Malcolm Arnold: a catalogue."

London, Faber Music, 1986, pp.13-26.

An account, with musical examples of Arnold's music and its characteristics.

B129.   Cole, H. "Malcolm Arnold: a biographical note."
In 65th birthday concert programme (1986).

A thumbnail sketch of Arnold's life.

B130.   Cole, H. "Malcolm Arnold: an introduction to his music."
London, Faber Music, 1989.

A major introduction which puts Arnold and his music into perspective and provides a comprehensive and perceptive commentary on his work.

B131.   Cole, H. "Malcolm Arnold at 60."
Music and Musicians, 29 (October 1981), pp.9-11.

An assessment of Arnold's unique position in English music.

B132.   Cole, H. "Oh! listen to the band."
Country Life, 31 October 1974, p.1274.

A sketch of the National Brass Band Championship Finals when Arnold's *Fantasy for Brass Band* was played as the test-piece. SEE: W298

B133.   Craggs, S.R. "Arnold listed."
Musical Times, 128 (May 1987), pp.267+269.

A review of Alan Poulton's catalogue.

B134.   Crankshaw, G. "Double Piano Concerto."
Music and Musicians, 18 (October 1969), pp.55-56.

A description of Arnold's *Concerto for 2 pianos (3 hands) and Orchestra*, first heard at a Promenade Concert. SEE: W29

B135.   Crankshaw, G. "Malcolm Arnold at 70."
Musical Opinion, 115 (February 1992), p.67.

An account of the Arnold 70th birthday concert.

B136.   Crichton, R. "Music in London."
         Musical Times, 110 (October 1969), p.1053.

         Mention of *Concerto for 2 pianos (3 hands) and Orchestra*,
         played at the Promenade Concerts. SEE: W29

B137.   Culot, H. "Arnold: Symphonies 1 and 2."
         British Music Society Newsletter, no.70 (June 1996), p.244.

         A review of the Naxos recording 8.553406. SEE: D70, D71

B138.   Culot, H. "Arnold Symphonies 5 and 6."
         British Music Society Newsletter, no.69 (March 1996), pp.220-
         221.

         A review of the Chandos recording CHAN 9385. SEE: D74,
         D75

B139.   Culot, H. "Arnold: Symphony No.9."
         British Music Society Newsletter, no.71 (September 1996),
         p.269.

         A review of the Naxos recording 8.553540 which is "warmly
         recommended." SEE: D78

B140.   Culot, H. [Dallas Wind Symphony]
         British Music Society Newsletter, no.70 (June 1996), p.244.

         Comments on Reference Recording RR 66 CD
         SEE: D23, D25, D37, D40, D46, D47, D51, D52, D79, D89

B141.   Culot, H. "Malcolm Arnold."
         British Music Society Newsletter, no.67 (September 1995),
         p.159.

         A review of Koch International 3 7162-2. SEE: D1, D5, D20,
         D22, D55, D60, D64, D80, D81, D82, D85, D86, D88

B142.   Culot, H. "Malcolm Arnold."
         British Music Society Newsletter, no.68 (December 1995),
         pp.188-189.

A review of ASV CDDCA922. SEE: D8, D9, D21, D29, D65, D83

B143.   Culot, H. "Sounds around."
British Music Society Newsletter, no.57 (March 1993), pp.178-179.

Views on the Chandos recording CHAN 9112. SEE: D56, D57

B144.   Culot, H. "Sounds around."
British Music Society Newsletter, no.63 (September 1994), p.63.

A review of Reference Recording RR 48 CD. SEE: D2, D6, D26, D63, D68

B145.   Culot, H. "Sounds around."
British Music Society Newsletter, no.64 (December 1994), p.83.

A review of the Chandos recording CHAN 9290. SEE: D72 , D73

B146.   Culot, H. "Sounds around."
British Music Society Newsletter, no.65 (March 1995), p.108.

An account of the Conifer recording CDCF 240. SEE: D4, D17, D39, D71

B147.   Dankworth, J. "Tribute."
In 65th birthday concert programme (1986).

A birthday tribute.

B148.   Davies, P.M. " Tribute."
In 65th birthday concert programme (1986).

A birthday tribute.

B149.   Dawney, M. "National Youth Orchestra."
Musical Opinion, 114 (April 1991), p.131.

Impressions of Arnold's *Symphony No.7* after a performance by the National Youth Orchestra of Great Britain. SEE: W73

B150. [Day, A.] "Music Master."
       The Lady, 15 October 1996, pp.48-49.

       Brief biographical details, written to celebrate his 75th birthday,
       and a conversation with the composer.

B151. Deas, S. "The Exhaustion of Music."
       Country Life, 11 July 1968, p.77.

       A discussion about Arnold's *Sixth Symphony*. SEE: W72

B152. Denton, D. "Arnold's New Symphony."
       Music and Musicians, 16 (August 1968), p.42.

       A review of the *Sixth Symphony's* first performance in Sheffield.
       SEE: W72

B153. Duarte, J. "Orchestral."
       Gramophone, 65 (August 1987), p.282.

       A record review.

B154. Duarte, J. "Orchestral."
       Gramophone, 68 (April 1991), p.1821.

       A review of Decca 430 233-2DH. SEE: D11

B155. Duarte, J. "Orchestral."
       Gramophone, 71 (July 1993), p.34.

       A review of EMI CDC7 54661-2. SEE: D11

B156. Dunnett, R. "Arnold."
       BBC Music Magazine, 5 (January 1997), p.84.

       A review of the EMI recording (CDM 5661202) of *Homage to
       the Queen*. SEE: D43

B157. Dunnett, R. "Malcolm Arnold: Freeman of Northampton."
       Musical Opinion, 113 (March 1990), pp.86-87.

       A feature on the composer.

B158.   Eastaugh, K. "The right man for a fantastic finale!"
        Daily Mirror, 24 September 1969, p.9.

        A brief appreciation of Arnold's life and music.

B159.   Edwards, A. "Arnold with Arnold."
        Gramophone, 73 (July 1995), p.27.

        Mention of the pieces for clarinet, recorded by Emma Johnson.

B160.   Elder, J. "For St Cecilia Malcolm Arnold writes a new Toy Symphony."
        Music and Musicians, 6 (November 1957), p.19.

        Details about the *Toy Symphony*. SEE: W79

B161.   Elliot, J.H. "Overture: Tam O'Shanter."
        Programme note of the first performance.

        BBC Promenade Concert, 16 August 1955. SEE.:W76

B162.   Ellis, D. "Tribute."
        In 65th birthday concert programme (1986).

        A birthday tribute.

B163.   Fawkes, R. "Heights and depths."
        Classical Music, no.438, 19 October 1991, p.11.

        An appreciation of the composer on his 70th birthday.

B164.   "Fiona." "Malcolm Arnold in harmony with Scotland."
        Dundee Courier and Advertiser, 28 May 1987, p.3.

        Details of the 1987 Perth Festival when Arnold was the featured
        composer.

B165.   Fisher, P. "Light out of darkness."
        Classic CD, no.11 (March 1991), pp.31+33-34.

        A profile of the composer.

B166.   Fisher, P. "Old Wild Child is back in tune."
        The Sunday Telegraph, 6 October 1991, p.7.

A celebratory article describing "....the belated return to grace of composer Malcolm Arnold."

B167. Fletcher, A. [Scottish Dances].
        Music Teacher, 61 (April 1982), p.12.

        An analysis for students undertaking O-level music. SEE: W43

B168. Fluck, A. "Festival of Youth."
        Composer, no.25 (Autumn 1967), p.16.

        Mention of a concert when Arnold's *Little Suite, No.2* (Opus 78) was performed by children. SEE: W49

B169. Ford, C. "Malcolm Arnold."
        The Guardian, 17 April 1971, p.8.

        An appreciation of the composer's life and music.

B170. Foreman, L. "Lyrita returns."
        Gramophone, 68 (November 1990), p.906.

        An article describing Lyrita recordings with mention of Arnold.

B171. Foss, H. "New works at Cheltenham."
        Hallé Magazine, June 1951, pp.5-11.

        A survey of works performed at the 1951 Cheltenham Festival with mention of Arnold's *First Symphony*. SEE: W67

B172. Frank, A. "Radio Music."
        Musical Times, 94 (December 1953), pp.569-570.

        Mention of the first *String Quartet*. SEE: W113

B173. G-F., C. "B.B.C. Symphony Orchestra."
        Musical Opinion, 84 (December 1960), pp.143-144.

        Views on the first performance of Arnold's *4th Symphony*. SEE: W70

B174. F-F., C. "Royal Liverpool Philharmonic Orchestra."
        Musical Opinion, 81 (July 1958), p.233.

A review of the concert when Arnold's *3rd Symphony* was first performed. SEE: W69

B175.   Gibson, L. "Concert review."
         Clarinet, 2, no.2 (1975), p.20.

         A review of the concert when Arnold's *2nd Clarinet Concerto* was first performed. SEE: W16

B176.   Gilardino, A. "Contemporary guitar music in Great Britain."
         Fronimo, 1/5 (October 1973), pp. 8-14.

         An article (in Italian) surveying British guitar music with mention of works by Arnold.

B177.   Goddard, S. "A young British symphonist."
         The Listener, 51 (4 February 1954), p.237.

         A survey of Arnold's music with particular mention of his symphonies to date.

B178.   Goddard, S. "Malcolm Arnold."
         Canon, 15(April 1962), pp.11-12.

         A biography of the composer.

B179.   Gomme, A. and Pirie, P.J. "Correspondence: Normality in Music."
         Music Review, 18 (February 1957), pp.87-88.

         A discussion with mention of Arnold's music.

B180.   Goodwin, N. "Commentary."
         Music and Musicians, 19 (November 1970), p.33.

         Comments on Arnold's *Fantasy for Audience and Orchestra*. SEE: W37

B181.   Goodwin, N. "Malcolm Arnold's Second Symphony."
         Truth, 11 June 1954, p.754.

         Views on the *2nd Symphony*. SEE: W68

B182.   Gray, M. "Arnold's music is sure to entertain."

Richmond and Twickenham Times, 10 March 1962, p.15.

An appreciation of *The Dancing Master*. SEE: W1

B183.   Greenfield, E. "Arnold/ Walton."
        Gramophone 71 (January 1994), p.62.

        A review of Chandos CHAN 9148. SEE: D54

B184.   Greenfield, E. "Arnold: Clarinet Works."
        Gramophone, 73 (July 1995), p.43.

        A review of ASV CDDCA 922. SEE: D8, D9, D21, D29, D65,
        D83

B185.   Greenfield, E. [Arnold: Classic Recordings]
        Gramophone, 74 (November 1996), pp.76-77.

        A review of the BBC Radio Classics recording 15656 91817-2,
        issued to celebrate Arnold's 75th birthday.
        SEE: D13, D17, D18, D19, D26, D30, D33, D35, D53, D61,
        D66

B186.   Greenfield, E. "Arnold: Concertos."
        Gramophone, 67 (August 1989), p.293.

        A record review.

B187.   Greenfield, E. "Arnold: Dances."
        Gramophone, 68 (December 1990), p.1197.

        A review of Lyrita Conifer SRCD 201. SEE: D23, D24, D35,
        D36, D37, D58

B188.   Greenfield, E. "Arnold: Film Music."
        Gramophone, 70 (February 1993), pp.37-38.

        A review of Chandos CHAN 9100. SEE: D3, D41, D44, D67,
        D90

B189.   Greenfield, E. "Arnold: Orchestral Works."
        Gramophone, 70 (June 1992), p.37.

A review of Koch International Classics 37134-2. SEE: D18, D59, D61, D62

B190.   Greenfield, E. Arnold: Orchestral Works."
        Gramophone, 70 (December 1992). p.72.

        A review of Conifer CDCF 211. SEE: D16, D19, D45, D59

B191.   Greenfield, E. "Arnold: Overtures."
        Gramophone, 70 (June 1992), pp.37-38.

        A review of Reference Recordings RR 48 CD. SEE: D2, D6, D26, D63, D68

B192.   Greenfield, E. "Concertos."
        Gramophone, 71 (December 1993), p.61.

        A review of Conifer CDCF 228. SEE: D9, D10, D12, D14

B193.   Greenfield, E. "Malcolm Arnold."
        The Guardian, 29 December 1965, p.5.

        A critic's reactions to a BBC radio portrait of the composer.

B194.   Greenfield, E. "Malcolm Arnold at the QEH."
        The Guardian, 27 April 1970, p.8.

        A review of a concert featuring Arnold's music.

B195.   Greenfield, E. "Norfolk notes."
        The Guardian, 7 July 1989, p.32.

        "In 1984 doctors told Malcolm Arnold he had two years to live. But the composer defied experts and is now back on prolific form." A report on Arnold's career and an examination of his recorded works.

B196.   Greenfield, E. "Orchestral."
        Gramophone, 71 (December 1993), p.60.

        A review of Hyperion CDA66643. SEE: D8, D9, D91

B197.   Greenfield, E. "R.C.M. Gala."

The Guardian, 1 February 1983, p.9.

An account of the concert when Arnold's *Trumpet Concerto* was first performed. SEE: W27

B198.   Greenfield, E. "Sounds of Dog-Fights."
         The Guardian, 29 April 1969, p.10.

         Details of the recording sessions at Denham when Arnold conducted the orchestra playing the soundtrack, composed by Walton, for *The Battle of Britain.* SEE: W166

B199.   Greenfield, E. "String Quartets."
         Gramophone, 70 (October 1992), p.124.

         A review of Chandos CHAN 9112. SEE: D56, D57

B200.   Greenfield, E. "[Symphony No.9]"
         Gramophone, 74 (April 1997), p.49.

         A review of Conifer Classics 75605 51273-2. SEE: D7, D31, D78

B201.   Greenhaigh, J. "Arnold's Guitar Concerto."
         Music on Musicians, 18 (June 1970), p.50.

         Comments on Arnold's *Guitar Concerto* and the first performance of his *Concerto for 28 players.* SEE: W19, W28

B202.   Greenhalgh, M. "A friend of music."
         Records and Recordings, 20 (August 1977), pp.24-25.

         A review of a new recording and interview with the composer.

B203.   Gregory, A. "Malcolm Arnold: an interview."
         Philharmonic Post, 6 (November - December 1951), pp.8-10.

         An early discussion with the composer.

B204.   Gregory, E. "The melody maker."
         Sounding Brass, 2 (July 1973), pp. 47-49.

         Arnold's views on his career and music.

B205.   Griffiths, P. "New music."
        Musical Times, 118 (July 1977), p.575.

        Details about Arnold's *Fantasy on a theme of John Field*. SEE:
        W38

B206.   Groves, C. "Foreword."
        In Poulton, A. "The Music of Malcolm Arnold: A catalogue."
        London, Faber Music, 1986, p.11.

        A brief welcome to Poulton's catalogue.

B207.   Groves, C. "Tribute."
        In 65th birthday concert programme (1986).

        A birthday tribute.

B208.   Hamburger, P. "The Cheltenham Festival."
        Music Review, 12 (November 1951), pp.318-319.

        Views on the first performance of *Symphony No.1*. SEE: W67

B209.   Hamburger, P. "Malcolm Arnold."
        Music Survey, 3 (June 1951), p.297.

        A brief review of the first performance of Arnold's *Sonata of
        Clarinet and Piano*. SEE: W124

B210.   Hanna, S.R. "Analysis and performance of music for unaccompanied
        bassoon by Malcolm Arnold, Gordon Jacob, Willson Osborne, George
        Perle and Vincent Persichetti.
        DMA Eastman School of Music (University of Rochester, New
        York), 1993.
        An examination of Arnold's *Fantasy for Bassoon* (W91)

B211.   Harrison, J, "English Dances, Set 2."
        Programme note for the first performance BBC Promenade
        Concert, 5 August 1952. SEE: W35

B212.   Harrison, M.. "E.C.O."
        Musical Times, 111 (June 1970), p.621.

        Views of an Arnold concert at the Queen Elizabeth Hall in

London.

B213.   Harrison, S. "Homage to Queens."
        John O'London's Weekly, 26 June 1953, p.5.

        Brief comments on Arnold's Coronation ballet. SEE: W6

B214.   Headington, C. "British Music for Clarinet and Piano."
        Gramophone, 70 (July 1993), p.47.

        A record review and general comments.

B215.   Headington, C. "Summer Music."
        Gramophone, 68 (January 1991), p.1386.

        A record review and views on the music.

B216.   Heyworth, P. "Study in contrasts: symphonies by Fricker and Arnold
        reveal different English styles."
        New York Times, 110 (Section 2), 4 December 1960, p.9.

        Discussion about the symphonies of Arnold and Peter Racine
        Fricker.

B217.   Higgins, T. "Arnold's Cello Concerto."
        Musical Opinion, 112 (July 1989), p.248.

        Notes on Arnold's *Cello Concerto* and its first performance.
        SEE: W58

B218.   Hofacre, M.J. "The use of tenor trombone in 20th century brass quintet
        music."
        D.M.A. dissertation, University of Oklahoma, 1986.

        Arnold's *Quintet for Brass* is used as one of the examples in the
        dissertation to illustrate the challenges of technique in
        performance. SEE: W309

B219.   Hold, T. "CD reviews."
        Musical Times, 134 (January 1993), p.42.

        A review of the compact disc of Arnold's *String Quartets Nos 1
        and 2*. SEE: D56, D57

B220.   Houston, D. "Back in Watford."
　　　　　Gramophone, 70 (June 1992), p.13.

　　　　　A report from a recording session with Malcolm Arnold.

B221.   Hughes-Jones, L. "Arnold premiere."
　　　　　Music and Musicians, 10 (May 1962), p.41.

　　　　　An account of the first London performance of Arnold's *Quintet for Brass*. SEE: W309

B222.   Hussey, D. "The Cheltenham Festival."
　　　　　Musical Times, 98 (September 1957), p.506.

　　　　　A review of the 1957 Cheltenham Festival with members of Arnold's *2nd Horn Concerto*. SEE: W22

B223.   Hutchings, E. "Leeds Castle Gala Finale."
　　　　　Musical Opinion, 110 (December 1987), p.373.

　　　　　Impressions of the *4 Irish Dances* after their first performance. SEE: W42

B224.   J., P.O. "Hit tunes in new work at Festival."
　　　　　Gloucestershire Echo. 4, July 1961, p.7.

　　　　　A review of *Symphony No.5* and its first performance at Cheltenham. SEE: W71

B225.   Jacobs, A. "Arnold moves from the River Kwai to the Nativity."
　　　　　Reynolds News, 10 January 1960, p.13.

　　　　　Views of the *Song of Simeon*. SEE: W147

B226. Jacobs, A. "Cheltenham Festival."
　　　　　Musical Times, 92 (September 1951), pp.416-417.

　　　　　A review of the first performance of *Symphony No.1*. SEE: W67

B227.   Jacobs, A. "Here is a new name to watch."
　　　　　Reynolds News, 13 November 1960, p.10.

　　　　　Details of young composers, including Arnold, who, according to the writer, are "....up-and-coming."

B228.   Jacobs, A. "Malcolm Arnold's String Quartet No.1."
         Musical Times, 92 (December 1951), p.563.

         A review of the first performance. SEE: W113

B229.   Jacobs, A. "The Smoke in Kensington."
         Daily Express, 25 October 1948, p.3.

         A review of the concert when Arnold's overture *The Smoke* was
         given its first performance. SEE: W62

B230.   Jacobs, A. "Three Composers."
         Picture Post, 53 (29 December 1951), pp.28-29.

         A feature (with photographs) on Richard Arnell, Arnold and
         Peter Racine Fricker.

B231.   John, E. "Rivers of Music."
         Music and Letters, 33 (October 1952), p.371.

         Notes on the published score of the arrangement of Arnold's
         Concerto for clarinet and strings, arranged for clarinet and
         piano. SEE: W15

B232.   Jolly, J. (Ed.) "Arnold at 75."
         Harrow, Gramophone Publications Ltd., 1996.

         A birthday tribute to Arnold which contains interviews, a survey
         of his music and a complete 1996 concerts listing.

B233.   Jones, P. "Tribute."
         In 65th birthday concert programme (1986).

         A birthday tribute.

B234.   Keller, H. "The half-year's new music."
         Music Review, 15 (February 1954), pp.56-57.

         Mention of Arnold's *2nd Violin Sonata* and the *2nd Symphony*.

         SEE: W68, W123

B235.   Keller, H. "The half-year's new music."
        Music Review, 16 (August 1955), pp.228-229.

        Mention of Arnold's *Concerto for flute and strings.* SEE: W17

B236.   Keller, H. "Malcolm Arnold's 3rd Symphony."
        London Musical Events, 13 (January 1958), pp 20-21.

        Views on the *3rd Symphony.* SEE: W69

B237.   Keller, H. "The new in review."
        Music Review, 17 (November 1956), pp. 333-335.

        Mention of Arnold's *Symphony No.2* SEE: W68

B238.   Keller, H. "The Secular Chorale."
        Musical Opinion, 79 (May 1956), p.481.

        Views on Arnold's overture *Tam O' Shanter.* SEE: W76

B239.   Kennedy, M. "Arnold: Chamber Works."
        Gramophone, 66 (January 1989), p.1169.

        A record review with views on the music.

B240.   Kennedy. M. "Arnold's 8th Symphony."
        The Daily Telegraph. 3 October 1981, p.11.

        Views on the *Eighth Symphony* and its first UK performance.
        SEE: W74

B241.   Keys, I. "Reviews of Music."
        Music and Letters, 30 (April 1949), p.188.

        Reviews of the published scores of the *Sonatina for flute and
        piano*, and *Variations on a Ukrainian Folksong.* SEE: W125,
        W138

B242.   Keys, I. "Reviews of Music."
        Music and Letters, 33 (April 1952), pp.180-181.

        A review of the printed score of Arnold's *String Quartet No.1.*
        SEE: W113

B243. Keys, I. "Reviews of Music."
>   *Music and Letters*, 33 (April 1952), pp.266-267.

>   A review of the printed score of Arnold's second suite of *English Dances*. SEE: W35

B244. Keys, I. "Reviews of Music."
>   *Music and Letters*, 35 (January 1954), p.74.

>   A review of the published score of Arnold's *Sonatina for recorder and piano*. SEE: W127

B245. Keys, I. "Reviews of Music."
>   *Music and Letters*, 35 (July 1954), p.265.

>   A review of the published score of *Arnold's Concerto for flute and strings*. SEE: W17

B246. Keys, I. "Reviews of Music."
>   *Music and Letters*, 36 (January 1955), pp. 102-103.

>   Views on the printed score of Arnold's *Trio*. SEE: W134

B247. Lambton, C. "Arnold: Symphony No.9."
>   *BBC Music Magazine*, 4 (June 1996). p.78.

>   A review of the Naxos recording 8.553540. SEE: D78

B248. Loppert, M, "Reports: Aldeburgh."
>   *Musical Times*, 117 (August 1976), pp.674-675.

>   A report on the first performance of new works including Arnold's *2nd String Quartet*. SEE: W114

B249. Loveland, K. "Cheltenham."
>   *Musical Times*, 120 (September 1979), p.755.

>   Views on Arnold's *Symphony for Brass*. SEE: W314

B250. Loveland, K. "Malcolm Arnold's success."
>   *South Wales Argus*, 18 July 1957, p.6.

>   Impressions of the composer at the Cheltenham Music Festival.

B251.   Loveland, K. "Wales: Six for Severn."
        Music and Musicians, 15 (March 1967), p.44.

        A description of the *Severn Bridge Variations* to which Arnold
        contributed. SEE: W77

B252.   Macdonald, M. "Arnold: Orchestral Works."
        Gramophone, 67 (March 1990), p.1595.

        A record review with comments on the music.

B253.   Macdonald, M. "Arnold: Symphonies."
        Gramophone, 68 (June 1990), p.41.

        A review of EMI Studio CDM7 63368-2. SEE: D53, D71, D74

B254.   Macdonald, M. "Orchestral."
        Gramophone, 63 (September 1985), p.333.

        A record review.

B255.   Mann, W. "Jazz in new symphony."
        The Times, 1 July 1968, p.8.

        Views on the *6th Symphony*. SEE: W72

B256.   March, I. "Arnold: Dances."
        Gramophone, 68 (October 1990), p.731.

        A record review and comments on the music.

B257.   March, I. [Arnold: Dances]
        Gramophone, 74 (October 1996), p.47.

        A review of the Naxos recording 8.553526. SEE: D23, D24,
        D35, D36, D37, D38

B258.   March, I. "Arnold on Brass."
        Gramophone, 71 (December 1993), p.61.

        A review of Conifer CDCF 222. SEE: D23, D24, D27, D35,
        D37, D52

B259.   March, I. "Arnold: Orchestral Works."
         Gramophone, 69 (October 1991), p.73.

         A record review.

B260.   March, I. "Arnold: Orchestral Works."
         Gramophone, 71 (February 1994), p.36.

         A review of Conifer CDCF 224. SEE: D32, D69, D75, D79

B261.   March, I. "Arnold: Orchestral Works."
         Gramophone, 72 (December 1994), p.74.

         A review of Conifer CDCF 240. SEE: D4, D17, D39, D71

B262.   March, I. [Arnold: Orchestral Works]
         Gramophone, 74 (December 1996), pp.68-69.

         A review of Conifer Classics recording 75605 51258-2. SEE:
         D72, D73

B263.   March, I. "Arnold: Piano Works."
         Gramophone, 72 (February 1995), pp.70-71.

         A review of Koch International Classics 37162-2. SEE: D1, D5,
         D20, D22, D55, D60, D64, D80, D81, D82, D85, D84, D88

B264   March, I. "Arnold: Symphonies."
         Gramophone, 72 (March 1995), p.37.

         A review of Chandos CHAN 9335. SEE: D70, D71

B265.   March, I. [Arnold: Symphonies]
         Gramophone, 73 (December 1995), p.72.

         A review of the Chandos recording CHAN 9385. SEE: D74,
         D75

B266.   March, I. [Arnold: Symphonies]
         Gramophone, 74 (May 1996), pp.52-53.

         A review of the Naxos recording 8.553406. SEE: D70, D71

B267.   March, I. [Arnold: Symphonies]
         Gramophone, 74 (October 1996), pp.46-47.

         A review of the Conifer Classics recording 75605 51257-2.
         SEE: D70, D74

B268.   March, I. [Arnold: Symphonies]
         Gramophone, 72 (April 1995), p.46.

         A record review and comments on the music.

B269.   March, I. "Arnold: Symphony No.4."
         Gramophone, 68 (November 1990), p.973.

         A review of Lyrita./Conifer SRCD 200. SEE: D73

B270.   March, I. "Arnold: Symphonies 3 and 4."
         Gramophone, 72 (September 1994), p.44.

         A review of Chandos CHAN 9290. SEE: D72, D73

B271.   March, I. "Arnold: Symphony No.9."
         Gramophone, 74 (May 1996), p.53.

         A review of the Naxos recording 8.553540, together with an
         interview with the composer. SEE: D78

B272.   March, I. "Collector's Corner."
         Gramophone, 72 (June 1994), p.124.

         Mention of recording 09026 61598-2. SEE: D11

B273.   March, I. "Much loved music."
         Gramophone, 65 (November 1987), pp.715-716.

         Views on Arnold's music and a record review.

B274.   March, I. "Orchestral"
         Gramophone, 68 (March 1991), p.1657.

         A review of Conifer CDCF 177. SEE: D76, D77

B275.   Mason, C. "Malcolm Arnold's Third Symphony."

The Manchester Guardian, 10 December 1957, p.4.

Analysis of and views on Arnold's *Third Symphony*. SEE: W69

B276.   Mason, C. "R. B.A. Galleries."
          Musical Times, 92 (May 1951), p.229.

          An account of the first performance of Arnold's *Sonata for clarinet and piano*. SEE: W124

B277.   Mason, C. "Reviews of Music."
        Music and Letters, 36 (July 1955), pp.303-304.

        A review of the published score of Arnold's *Sinfonietta No.1*. SEE: W59

B278.   Mason, E. "Lessons after school."
        Music and Musicians, 11 (July 1963), p.41.

        A review of the second Farnham Festival which included Arnold's *Little Suite No.2*. SEE: W49

B279.   Maycock, R. "Nearly New."
        Music and Musicians, 22 (December 1973), pp.71-72.

        Reflections on the first London performance of Arnold's *2nd Flute Concerto*. SEE: W18

B280.   Mellers, W. "Records."
        Musical Times, 132 (July 1991), pp.350-351.

        Views on the Lyrita recording of the *Second Symphony*.

B281.   Mellor, D. "What about Arnold?"
        The Spectator, 7 December 1991, pp.41-42.

        A plea that "it is time for one of our great contemporary composers to receive his due."

B282.   Menuhin, Y. "Tribute."
        In 65th birthday concert programmes (1986).

        A birthday tribute.

B283.   Miller, S. W. "Analysis of Sir Malcolm Arnold's Tam O'Shanter, based on the poem by Robert Burns."
D.M.A. dissertation, University of Washington, 1970.

A useful analysis of the work. SEE: W76

B284.   Mills, H. "On first hearing..."
Making Music, no.64 (Summer 1967), p.15.

Impressions about the first performance of Arnold's *Little Suite No.2 for Brass*. SEE: W305

B285.   Mitchell, D. "Instrumental."
Musical Times, 97 (June 1956), p.317.

A review of the first performance of Arnold's *Piano Trio*. SEE: W135

B286.   Mitchell, D. "Malcolm Arnold."
Musical Times, 96 (August 1955), pp.410-413.

A survey of Arnold's life and music with musical examples and a list of works.

B287.   Mitchell, D. "Some first performances."
Musical Times, 94 (December 1953), p.576.

Mention of the first performance of Arnold's *2nd Sonata for Violin and Piano*. SEE: W123

B288.   Mitchell, D. "Some first performances."
Musical Times, 95 (April 1954), pp.201-202.

A review of the *First String Quartet's* first performance. SEE: W113

B289.   Mitchell, D. "Some first performances."
Musical Times, 95 (July 1954), p.382.

Views on Arnold's *2nd Symphony* after its first London performance. SEE: W69

B290.   Mitchell, D. "Some first performances."

Musical Times, 96 (May 1955), p.266.

Views on the first London performance of Arnold's Sinfonietta (*No.1*). SEE: W59

B291. Mitchell, D. "Tribute."
In 65th birthday concert programme (1986).

A birthday tribute.

B292. Morgan, T. "A Catalogue."
Composer, 90 (Spring 1987), p.22.

A review of the Poulton catalogue, published by Faber.

B293. Myers, R. H. "British Music."
Canon, 14 (Jan-Feb 1961), pp.107-108.

Views on Arnold's *Symphony No.4*. SEE: W70

B294. Noble, J. "Cheltenham."
Musical Times, 102 (August 1961), p.498.

A review of the *5th Symphony's* first performance. SEE: W71

B295. Notcutt, A. "London orchestral anniversary marked as concerts multiply."
Musical Courier, 148 (1 November 1953), p.6.

Details of the concert when Arnold's *Flourish of a 21st birthday* was first performed. SEE: W300

B296. O'Loughlin, N. "Brass ensemble."
Musical Times, 126 (January 1985), p.34.

A review of the published score of Arnold's *Symphony for Brass*. SEE: W314

B297. Ormerod, J.   "Nallen, Lindsay String Quartet, Manchester, 15 November."
Recorder Magazine, 12, no.1 (1992), p.6.

Details about the first UK performance of Arnold's *Fantasy for*

Recorder and String Quartet, (Opus 140). SEE: W100

B298.   Ottaway, H. "British Songs."
        Musical Times, 107 (December 1966), p.1081.

        A review of the score of Arnold's *Five William Blake Songs*.
        SEE: W152

B299.   Ottaway, H."English."
        Musical Times, 109 (July 1968), p.659.

        A review of the score of Arnold's *Four Cornish Dances*. SEE:
        W41

B300.   Ottaway, H. "Rubbra conducted by Arnold."
        Radio Times, 28 July 1966, p.53.

        Reflections on both composers with particular mention of the
        concert conducted by Arnold.

B301.   Palmer, C. "Malcolm Arnold."
        Gramophone, 69 (October 1991), pp.53-54.

        A 70th birthday tribute.

B302.   Payne, A. "Composers in the rostrum."
        Music and Musicians, 13 (September 1964), p.24.

        An account of a concert at the Victoria and Albert Museum,
        London, when Arnold conducted the first London performance of
        his *Concerto for 2 violins and string orchestra*. SEE: W30

B303.   Peterborough. "In the blood."
        The Daily Telegraph, 21 October 1971, p.18.

        A mention of Arnold's 50th birthday with details of his musical
        forebears on his mother's side.

B304.   Peyton, J. "Tribute."
        In 65th birthday concert programme (1986).

        A birthday tribute.

B305.   Pirie, P.J. "British."
         Musical Times, 126 (March 1985), p.164.

         Mention of some new printed Arnold scores.

B306.   Pirie, P.J. "Broadcasting."
         Musical Times, 104 (May 1963), p.347.

         A review of a concert given by the BBC Northern Orchestra and
         conducted by Arnold.

B307.   Pirie, P.J. "Records: Hoddinott, Fricker and Arnold."
         Music and Musicians, 26 (February 1978), pp.35-36.

         Comparisons between the three composers, including Arnold.

B308.   Porter, A. "Malcolm Arnold."
         London Musical Events, 9 (February 1954), pp.17-18.

         A sketch about the composer and his music.

B309.   Porter, A. "New music at the Proms."
         London Music, 9 (August 1954), p.32.

         A review of the first performance of Arnold's *Concerto for
         Harmonica and Orchestra*. SEE: W20

B310.   Porter, A. "The Open Window."
         Opera, 13 (February 1962), p.140.

         A report about the performance of Arnold's opera, *The Open
         Window*, at Morley College. SEE: W3

B311.   Porter, A. "Two British Symphonies."
         Musical Times, 101 (December 1960), p.766.

         A review of the concert (at the Royal Festival Hall), when
         Arnold's 4th Symphony and Peter Racine Fricker's 3rd
         Symphony were featured.

B312.   Poulton, A. "The Music of Malcolm Arnold: A catalogue."
         London, Faber Music, 1986.

A useful documentation of Arnold's output up to 1986.

B313.   Preston, R. "Light and Shade."
        Music and Musicians, 37 (April 1989), pp.42-43.

        A profile of the composer.

B314.   Pritchard, J. "Tribute."
        In 65th birthday concert programme (1986).

        A birthday tribute.

B315.   R.,H.S. "The Royal Ballet."
        Musical Opinion, 84 (October 1960), p.9.

        Views on Arnold's ballet *Sweeney Todd*. SEE. W9

B316.   Rayment, M. "Malcolm Arnold's debut with SNO."
        Glasgow Herald, 2 July 1973, p.2.

        Details of the concert which contained two works by Arnold who
        conducted the Scottish National Orchestra for the first time.

B317.   Rayment, M."Malcolm Arnold's Symphony...."
        Musical Express, 7 December 1961, p.2.

        Views on Arnold's music.

B318.   Rayment, M. "Promenade Concerts."
        Musical Times, 94 (September 1953), p.422.

        Reflections on the 1953 Henry Wood Promenade Concerts when
        Arnold's *Concerto for Piano Duet and Strings* was first
        performed. SEE: W25

B319.   Rayment, M. "Promenade Concerts."
        Musical Times, 96 (November 1955), p.601.

        Details about the first performance of *Tam O'Shanter*. SEE:
        W76

B320.   Raynor, H. "The Promenade Concerts 1969."
        Music Review, 31, no.1 (1970), p.82.

A survey of the Promenade Concerts (1969 Season) with mention of Arnold's *Concerto for 2 Pianos (3 hands) and Orchestra.* SEE: W29

B321.   Rees, C.B. "Impressions: Malcolm Arnold."
         London Musical Events, 10 (August 1955). pp.15-16.

         A sketch of the composer and his work.

B322.   Reid, C. "Tonight it's bongo night."
         Daily Mail, 2 November 1960, p.8.

         A brief interview with the composer.

B323.   Reynolds, M. "Fantasy for Audience."
         Music and Musicians, 19 (November 1970), p. 58.

         Comments on Arnold's *Fantasy for Audience and Orchestra.* SEE: W37

B324.   Richards, D. "The contemporary scene."
         Musical Opinion, 100 (January 1977), pp.181,183-184.

         A survey of British music with mention of Arnold and recent works.

B325.   Richards, D. "Croydon."
         Music and Musicians, 21 (July 1973), p.76.

         Notes on the concert when *The Fair Field* was first performed in Croydon. SEE: W36

B326.   Richards, D. "Northern Sinfonia."
         Music and Musicians, 20 (January 1972), p.62.

         An account of the first performance of Arnold's *Viola Concerto* in Newcastle-upon-Tyne. SEE: W31

B327.   Richards, D. "Of the select few."
         Music and Musicians, 15 (May 1967), p.44.

         A review of a concert when Arnold conducted the Royal Philharmonic Orchestra at the Camden Festival.

B328.   Ritchie, C. "The Arnold-Lean Trilogy."
        From Silents to Satellite, 10 (Autumn 1991), pp.26-32.

        Details of the three films directed by David Lean, with music by Arnold: *The Sound Barrier, Hobson's Choice* and *Bridge on the River Kwai*. SEE: W172, W200, W247

B329.   Ritchie, C. "A Filmography/discography of Malcolm Arnold."
        Soundtrack! No.26 [1986], pp.18-23.

        Useful lists of Arnold's music for films.

B330.   Ritchie, C. "Malcolm Arnold just writes what he would like to hear."
        Soundtrack! No.27 [1987], pp.5-9.

        A detailed interview with the composer.

B331.   Robertson, A. "Concerto for Piano Duet and Strings."
        Programme note for the first London performance, BBC Promenade Concert, 31 July 1953. SEE: W25

B332.   Rose, B. "Reviews of Music."
        Music and Letters, 33 (January 1952), p.95.

        Mention of the *Sonatinas for clarinet and piano, and oboe and piano* and their published scores. SEE: W124, W126

B333.   Rose, B. "Review of Music."
        Music and Letters, 34 (January 1953), pp. 81-82.

        A review of the published score of Arnold's *Three Shanties*. SEE: W132

B334.   Rostron, M. "Philharmonic Concerto."
        British Music Society Newsletter, no.66 (June 1995), p.131.

        A review of the book on Arnold and his music by Piers Burton-Page.

B335.   Rothschild, L.de. "Tribute."
        In 65th birthday concert programme (1986).

        A birthday tribute.

B336.   Rutland, H. "Song of Simeon."
        Musical Times, 101 (February 1960), p.101.

        Impressions of the *Song of Simeon* and its first performance.
        SEE: W147

B337.   Rye, M. "Arnold: Symphonies 1 and 2."
        BBC Music Magazine, 4 (April 1996), p.76.

        A review of the Naxos recording 8.553406. SEE: D70, D71

B338.   S., P.H. "Baton change."
        The Times, 4 November 1970, p.12.

        The composer's reasons for undertaking less conducting.

B339.   Sadie, S. "Music in London."
        Musical Times, 111 (November 1970), p.1121.

        Mention of Arnold's *Fantasy for Audience and Orchestra*.
        SEE: W37

B340.   Sadie, S. "The Proms."
        Musical Times, 109 (September 1968), pp.826-827.

        A review of Promenade Concerts and mention of *Peterloo*, the
        composer conducting. SEE: W51

B341.   Sadie, S. "Yehudi Menuhin's farewell to Bath Festival."
        The Times, 1 July 1968. p.7.

        Details of Menuhin's last concerts and a performance with Igor
        Oistrakh of Arnold's *Concerto for Two Violins and String
        Orchestra*. SEE: W30

B342.   Sanders, A. "Compact Disc Round-up."
        Gramophone, 66 (September 1988), p.492.

        A record review.

B343.   Schafer, M. "Malcolm Arnold."
        In his "British Composers in Interview," London, Faber, 1963,
        pp.147-154.

An interview with the composer.

B344.   Scott-Maddocks, D. "Diverting Arnold."
        Music and Musicians, 10 (May 1962), p.43.

        An account of the concert, in the Royal Festival Hall, when
        Arnold's *Divertimento No.2* was first performed in London.
        SEE: W33

B345.   Sear, H.G. "English music."
        Philharmonic Post, 7 (May-June 1954), p.32.

        A brief survey of English music with mention of Malcolm
        Arnold.

B346.   Senior, E. "Malcolm Arnold."
        Music and Musicians, 9 (February 1961), p.24.

        Impressions of *Symphony No.4*. SEE: W70

B347.   Shawe-Taylor, D. "Symphonies High Spirits."
        The Sunday Times, 4 November 1960, p.34.

        A review of the composer's work and impressions of the *Fourth
        Symphony*. SEE: W70

B348.   Simmons, D. "London Music."
        Musical Opinion, 93 (October 1969), p.4.

        Brief observations on Arnold's *Concerto for 2 Pianos (3 hands)
        and Orchestra*. SEE: W29

B349.   Simmons, D. "London Music."
        Musical Opinion, 94 (October 1970), pp.6-7.

        A review of the last night concert at the 1970 Promenade
        Concerts with mention of Arnold's *Fantasy of Audience and
        Orchestra*.
        SEE: W37

B350.   Simmons, D. "London Music."
        Musical Opinion, 95 (February 1972), p.232.

Impressions of *Symphony No.5* after its first London performance. SEE: W71

B351. Simmons, D. "London Music."
Musical Opinion, 97 (July 1974), pp.422-423+.

Mention of the premiers of Arnold's *Symphony No. 7*, conducted by the composer at the Royal Festival Hall. SEE: W73

B352. Sitwell, F. "Tribute."
In 65th birthday concert programme (1986).

A birthday tribute.

B353. Snook, P. "Peevish Puck of British Music."
Fanfare, 10, no.2 (1986), pp.85-88.

A description of the composer and his recordings.

B354. Spence, K. "Television."
Musical Times, 110 (May 1969), p.518.

Mention of a BBC television film on Arnold and his music.

B355. Squibb, D. "Fairground bustle."
Croydon Advertiser, 4 May 1973, p.26.

Impressions of *The Fair Field* and its first performance. SEE: W36

B356. Stasiak, C. "The symphonies of Malcolm Arnold."
Tempo, nos 161/162 (June/September 1987), pp.85-90.

A study of the symphonies, together with musical examples.

B357. Stewart, A. "Malcolm Arnold."
Music Teacher, 68 (June 1989), pp.25-28.

A detailed survey of Arnold's life and music, together with a list of works.

B358. Stewart, A. "New Books Reviewed."
Music Teacher, 68 (August 1989), p.27.

A review of Hugo Cole's book on Arnold and his music.

B359.   Sutton, W. "Understanding music."
        Musical Times, 130 (December 1989), pp.748-749.

        A review of Hugo Cole's introduction to Arnold's music.

B360.   Swallow, J. "Malcolm Arnold at 70."
        Instrument, 46 (October 1991), pp.16-19.

        A birthday tribute.

B361.   T., A. "Meet Malcolm Arnold - composer extraordinary."
        Sheffield Telegraph, 10 March 1962, p.4.

        Impressions of the composer and his music.

B362.   Talbert, T. "Current Scores."
        Film Music, 17 (Fall-Winter 1957-1958), pp.13-14.

        A review of new film music, including Arnold's score for *Bridge
        on the River Kwai*. SEE: W172

B363.   Talley, H. "Review introduces Symphony by Malcolm Arnold."
        Musical America, 77 (1 Jan 1957), p.7.

        Views on the *Second Symphony* when first played in the USA by
        the Chicago Symphony Orchestra on 12/13/56. SEE: W68

B364.   Thackeray, R. "Orchestral."
        Musical Times, 117 (December 1976), pp.1016-1017.

        Mention of the European premiere of Arnold's *Second Clarinet
        Concerto*. SEE: W16

B365.   Thompson, K. "Malcolm Arnold."
        *Journal of the British Association of Symphonic Bands and
        Wind Ensembles*, 3 (Autumn 1984), pp.10-13+15

        A conversation with the composer.

B366.   Tierney, N. "Liverpool hails Shostakovitch."
        Music and Musicians, 10 (December 1961), p.31.

Details about the premiere of the re-worked and revised *Divertimento No.2*. SEE: W33

B367. Tooley, J. "Tribute."
        In 65th birthday concert programme (1986).

        A birthday tribute.

B368. Tracey, E. "Farnham: Schools Festival."
        Musical Times, 104 (July 1963), p.493.

        Details of a concert in Farnham Parish Church when Arnold's *Little Suite No.2* was first performed. SEE: W49

B369. Tranchell, P. "Review of Music."
        Music in Letters, 33 (October 1952), p.365.

        A review of the *Symphony No.1* and its published score. SEE: W67

B370. Vaughan, D. [Arnold's ballets]
        In his "Frederick Ashton and his Ballets"
        London, A. & C. Black, 1977, pp.270,274,304,433.

        Details of ballets with music by Arnold. SEE: W6 , W7

B371. W., R.V. "A black mark for putting a tune into a symphony."
        Richmond and Twickenham Times, 8 July 1961, p.14.

        Reflections on Arnold's *5th Symphony*. SEE: W71

B372. W., R.V. "Concerto for Phyllis and Cyril."
        Richmond and Twickenham Times, 16 October 1970, p.15.

        Mention of Arnold's *Concerto for Phyllis and Cyril*. SEE: W29

B373. Warrack, J. "Sweet Melancholy."
        Gramophone, 70 (September 1992), p.124.

        A record review.

B374. Waugh, A. "Faithful in his fashion."
        The Sunday Telegraph Magazine, no.1, 17 September 1995,

pp.18-19.

A report on a visit to the Arnold ménage in Norfolk.

B375.   "Westcountryman." "Cornish Bard."
        The Western Morning News, 5 January 1970, p.4.

        Details of awards given to the composer.

B376.   Westland, L. "Tribute."
        In 65th birthday concert programme (1986).

        A birthday tribute.

B377.   Widdicombe, G. "Aldeburgh."
        Musical Times, 114 (August 1973), p.820.

        A review of the *2nd Flute Concerto's* premiere. SEE: W18

B378.   Widdicombe, G. "Arnold at 50."
        The Financial Times, 18 October 1971, p.3.

        An appreciation written to celebrate the composer's 50th birthday.

B379.   Willey, E.L. "British clarinet concertos."
        Clarinet, 12, no,2 (1985), pp.14-17.

        A chronological survey of clarinet concertos, written by British composers, with mention to those by Arnold.

B380.   Williams, P. "N.S.B.B.A. celebrates."
        Music Teacher, 52 (July 1973), p.25.

        A description of the concert, organised by the National Schools Brass Band Association, when *Song of Freedom* was first performed. SEE: W145

B381.   Wilson, C. "Caliban remains only a demi-semi-devil."
        Daily Mail, 14 April 1954, p.6.

        Views of Arnold's music for *The Tempest*. SEE: W288

B382.   Wolfe, P. "Facing the music."
         What's on in London, 29 January 1960, p.20.

         Report of a talk given by the composer in London.

B383.   Wood, E.G. "Newcastle."
         Newcastle Times, 112 (December 1971), p.1194.

         Brief mention of Arnold's *Viola Concerto*, first performed at the
         Newcastle Festival. SEE: W31

B384.   Wright, A. "New Music."
         Music and Musicians, 4 (June 1956), p.36.

         A review of the score of the *John Clare Cantata*. SEE. W139

APPENDIX A
ALPHABETICAL LIST OF COMPOSITIONS

Numbers following each title (e.g., W133) refer to the "Works and Performances" section of this volume.

Africa - Texas Style. W157
Airways, W158
Albert RN, W159
Alien Orders, W160
Allegro in E minor for piano, W82
Angry silence, The, W161
Anniversary Overture (Opus 99), W11
Anthony and Cleopatra, W162
Avalanche Patrol, W163

Badgers Green, W164
Barretts of Wimpole Street, The, W165
Battle of Britain, The, W166
Beautiful County of Ayr, The, W167
Beautiful Stranger, W168
Beckus the Dandipratt (Opus 5), W12
Belles of St. Trinian's, The, W169
Blue Murder at St. Trinian's, W170
Boy and the Bridge, The, W171
Britannia Mews, W173

Candlemas Night, W275
Captain's Paradise, The, W174
Carnival of Animals (Opus 72), W13
Chalk Garden, The, W175
Channel Islands, W176
Charting the Seas, W177
Children's Suite for Piano (Opus 16), W83
Christmas Carols (arrangements), W316
Commonwealth Christmas Overture (Opus 64), W14
Concert Piece for Percussion , W84

Concerto [No.1] for Clarinet and Strings (Opus 20), W15
Concerto [No.2] for Clarinet and Orchestra (Opus 115), W16
Concerto for Flute and Strings (Opus 45), W17
Concerto [No.2] for Flute and Orchestra (Opus 111), W18
Concerto for Guitar and Chamber Orchestra (Opus 67), W19
Concerto for Harmonica and Orchestra (Opus 46), W20
Concerto [No.1] for Horn and Orchestra (Opus 11), W21
Concerto [No.2] for Horn and Strings (Opus 58), W22
Concerto for Oboe and Strings (Opus 39), W23
Concerto for Organ and Orchestra (Opus 47), W24
Concerto for Piano Duet and Strings (Opus 32), W25
Concerto for Recorder and Orchestra (Opus 133), W26
Concerto for Trumpet and Orchestra (Opus 125), W27
Concerto of Twenty-Eight Players (Opus 105), W28
Concerto for Two Pianos (3 Hands) and Orchestra (Opus 104), W29
Concerto of Two Violins and String Orchestra (Opus 77), W30
Concerto for Viola and Chamber Orchestra (Opus 108), W31
Constant Husband, The, W178
Contrasts (Opus 134), W151
Copenhagen, City of Towers, W179
Cotton - Lancashire's Time for Adventure, W180
Coupe des Alpes, W181
Curtain Up, W182

Dancing Master, The (Opus 34), W1
David Copperfield, W183
Day Dreams, W85
Deep Blue Sea, The W184
Devil on Horseback, W185
Divertimento [No.1] for Orchestra (Opus 1), W32
Divertimento [No.2] for Orchestra (Opus 24), W33
Divertimento for Wind Octet (Opus 137), W292
Divertimento for Wind Trio (Opus 37), W86
Dollars and Sense, W186
Double-Hoquet, W137
Drums for a Holiday, W187
Dunkirk, W188
Duo for Flute and Violin (Opus 10), W87
Duo for two B-flat Clarinets (Opus 135), W88
Duo for two Cellos (Opus 85), W89

ECA Productivity Team, W189
Eight Children's Pieces for Piano (Opus 36), W90

Electra (incidental music), W276
Electra (ballet, Opus 79), W5
English Dances [Set 1] (Opus 27), W34
English Dances [Set 2] (Opus 33), W35
Espionage, W277
EVWs, W190

Fair Field, The (Opus 110), W36
Fanfare - ABC TV Title Music, W278
Fanfare for a Festival, W293
Fanfare for a Royal Occasion, W294
Fanfare for Louis, W295
Fanfare for One, 80 Years Young, W296
[Fanfare for the Farnham Festival], W297
Fantasy for Audience and Orchestra (Opus 106), W37
Fantasy for Bassoon (Opus 86), W91
Fantasy for Brass Band (Opus 114a), W298
Fantasy for Cello (Opus 130), W92
Fantasy for Clarinet (Opus 87), W93
Fantasy for Flute (Opus 89), W94
Fantasy for Guitar (Opus 107), W95
Fantasy for Harp (Opus 117), W96
Fantasy for Horn (Opus 88), W97
Fantasy for Oboe (Opus 90), W98
Fantasy for Recorder (Opus 127), W99
Fantasy for Recorder and String Quartet (Opus 140), W100
Fantasy for Trombone (Opus 101), W101
Fantasy for Trumpet (Opus 100), W102
Fantasy for Tuba (Opus 102), W103
Fantasy on a theme of John Field for Piano and Orchestra (Opus 116), W38
Festival Overture (Opus 14), W39
Fifty Acres, W191
Fight for a Fuller Life, W192
First Lady, The, W279
Five Pieces for Violin and Piano (Opus 84), W104
Five William Blake Songs (Opus 66), W152
Flourish for a Battle (Opus 139), W299
Flourish for Orchestra (Opus 112), W40
Flourish for a 21st Birthday (Opus 44), W300
For Mr Pye an Island, W280
Four Cornish Dances (Opus 91), W41
Four Irish Dances (Opus 126), W42
Four Pieces for Chamber Ensemble, W105

Four Scottish Dances (Opus 59), W43
Four Welsh Dances (Opus 138), W44
Four Sided Triangle, W193
Frazers of Cabot Cove, The, W194
Gala Performance, W281
Gates of Power, W195
Grand Concerto Gastronomique (Opus 76), W45
Grand Fantasia ("Opus 973"), W106
Grand, Grand Overture, A (Opus 57), W46
Great St. Trinian's Train Robbery, W196

Haile Selassie, W107
Hard Times, W282
Hawick, Queen of the Border, W197
Henri Christophe, W2
Heroes of Telemark, The, W198
Hill in Korea, A, W199
HRH The Duke of Cambridge (Opus 60), W301
Hobson's Choice, W200
Hoffnung Fanfare, W302
Holly and the Ivy, The, W201
Homage to the Queen (Opus 42), W6
Home at Seven, W202
Home to Danger, W203
Hydrography, W204

I am a Camera, W205
Inn of the Sixth Happiness, The, W206
Inspector, The, W207
Invitation to the Dance, W208
Island, The, W209
Island in the Sun, W210
It started in Paradise, W211

John Clare Cantata (Opus 52), W139
Jolly Old Friar, W140
Julius Ceasar, W212

Katherine, Walking and Running, W108
Kensington Gardens, W153
Key, The, W213
Kingston Fanfare, W303

Larch Trees (Opus 3), W47
Leonora [Overture] No.4, W48
Let go For'ard, W214
Lion, The, W215
Little Suite [No.1] for Brass Band (Opus 80), W304
Little Suite [No.2] for Brass Band (Opus 93), W305
Little Suite [No.3] for Brass Band (Opus 131), W306
Little Suite [No.2] for Orchestra (Opus 78), W49
Local Newspapers, W216

Man of Africa, W217
Manx Suite (Opus 142), W50
March: Overseas (Opus 70), W307
Men and Machines, W218
Metropolitan Water Board, W219
Mining Review, W220
Motet-Marie Assumptio, W318
Music for You, W283

Night my Number Came Up, The, W221
Nine Hours to Rama, W222
1984, W223
No Highway, W224
No Love for Johnnie, W225
North Sea Strike, W226

Oil Review No.5, W227
On the Brow of Richmond Hill (arrangement), W319
On the Fiddle, W228
Only a Little Box of Soldiers, W320
Open Window, The (Opus 56), W3
Overture for Wind Octet, W109

Paddy's Nightmare, W284
Padstow Lifeboat, The (Opus 94), W308
Parasol, W285
Peacock in the Zoo, The, W141
Peterloo (Opus 97), W51
Phantasy for String Quartet, W110
Philharmonic Concerto (Opus 120), W52
Popular Birthday, W53
Port Afrique, W229
Power for All, W230

Powered Flight, W231
Prelude for Piano, W111
Prize of Gold, W232
Psalm 150 (Opus 25), W142
Pure Hell of St. Trinian's, W233
Purple Dust, W286

Quartet for Oboe and Strings (Opus 61), W112
Quartet for Strings [No.1] (Opus 23), W113
Quartet for Strings [No.2] (Opus 118), W114
Quintet for Brass (Opus 73), W309
Quintet [No.2] for Brass (Opus 132), W310
Quintet for Flute, Violin, Viola, Horn and Bassoon (Opus 7), W115
Quintet for Wind (Opus 2), W116

Railway Fanfare, W311
Reckoning, The, W234
Report on Steel, W235
Return of Odysseus, The (Opus 119), W143
Richmond, W312
Riddle of Japan, The, W236
Rinaldo and Armida (Opus 49), W47
Ringer, The, W237
Robert Kett Overture (Opus 141), W54
Roots of Heaven, The, W238
Roses Tattoo, W239
Royal Prologue, W287
Royal Tour - New Zealand, W240

St. Endellion Ringers, W144
Salute to Thomas Merritt (Opus 98), W55
Savile Centenary Fanfare, W313
Science of the Orchestra, W241
Sea Shall Not Have Them, The, W242
Serenade for Guitar and Strings (Opus 50), W56
Serenade for Small Orchestra (Opus 26), W57
Serenade in G for Piano, W117
Seven RAF Flashes, W243
Shakespearean Cello Concerto (Opus 136), W58
Sinfonietta [No.1] (Opus 48), W59
Sinfonietta [No.2] (Opus 65), W60
Sinfonietta [No.3] (Opus 81), W61
Sky West and Crooked, W244

Sleeping Tiger, The, W245
Smoke, The (Opus 21), W62
Solitaire, W8
Solomon and Sheba, W246
Sonata for Flute and Piano, W118
Sonata for Flute and Piano (Opus 121), W119
Sonata for Piano in B minor, W120
Sonata for Viola and Piano (Opus 17), W121
Sonata [No.1] for Violin and Piano (Opus 15), W122
Sonata [No.2] for Violin and Piano (Opus 43), W123
Sonatina for Clarinet and Piano (Opus 29), W124
Sonatina for Flute and Piano (Opus 19), W125
Sonatina for Oboe and Piano (Opus 28), W126
Sonatina for Recorder and Piano (Opus 41), W127
Song of Accounting Periods, The (Opus 103), W154
Song of Freedom (Opus 109), W145
Song of Praise (Opus 55), W146
Song of Simeon (Opus 69), W147
Sound Barrier, The, W247
Stolen Face, W248
Story of Gilbert and Sullivan, The, W249
Struggle for Oil, The, W250
Suddenly Last Summer, W251
Suite Bourgeoise, W128
Sunshine Overture, A (Opus 83), W63
Sussex Overture, A (Opus 31), W64
Sweeney Todd (Opus 68), W9
Symphonic Suite for Orchestra (Opus 12), W65
Symphony for Brass (Opus 123), W314
Symphony for Strings (Opus 13), W66
Symphony No.1 (Opus 22), W67
Symphony No.2 (Opus 40), W68
Symphony No.3 (Opus 63), W69
Symphony No.4 (Opus 71), W70
Symphony No.5 (Opus 74), W71
Symphony No.6 (Opus 95), W72
Symphony No.7 (Opus 113), W73
Symphony No.8 (Opus 124), W74
Symphony No.9 (Opus 128), W75

Tamahine, W252
Tam o'Shanter (Opus 51), W76
Tango in D (arrangement), W321

Tempest, The, W288
Terra Incognita, W253
Theme and Three Variations, W326
Theme and Variation for Orchestra, W77
Theme for Player's, W289
Thin Red Line, The, W254
This Christmas Night, W148
This Farming Business, W255
This is Britain, W256
Thomas Merritt - anthems and carols (arrangements), W322
Thomas Merritt: Coronation March (arrangement), W323
Three Fantasies for Piano (Opus 129), W129
Three Musketeers, The, W10
Three Pieces for Piano, W130
Three Pieces for Piano, W131
Three Shanties for Wind Quintet (Opus 4), W132
Tiger in the Smoke, W257
To Youth, W78
Toy Symphony, W79
Trapeze, W258
Trevelyan Suite (Opus 96), W133
Trieste: Problem City, W259
Trio for Flute, Viola and Bassoon (Opus 6), W134
Trio for Violin, Viola and Piano (Opus 54), W135
Tunes of Glory, W260
Turtle Drum, The (Opus 92), W290
Two Bagatelles for Piano (Opus 18), W136
Two Ceremonial Psalms (Opus 35), W149
Two John Donne Songs (Opus 114b), W155
Two Part-Songs, W150
Two Pieces for Piano, W137
Two RAF Flashes, W261
Two Sketches for Oboe and Piano, W327
Two Songs for Voice and Piano (Opus 8), W156

United Nations, W80
Up at the Villa, W4
Up for the Cup, W262

Value for Money, W263
Variations for Orchestra on a Theme of Ruth Gipps (Opus 122), W81
Variations on a Ukranian Folk Song (Opus 9), W138

War in the Air, W291
Water Music (Opus 82), W315
We Three Kings of Orient Are (arrangement), W324
Welcome the Queen, W264
When You Went Away, W265
Where Britain Stands, W266
Whistle Down The Wind, W267
Wicked as They Come, W268
Wildcats of St. Trinian's, The, W269
William Walton: Sonata for String Orchestra (arrangement), W325
Wings of Danger, W270
Woman for Foe, The, W271
Women in Our Time, W272

You Know What Sailors Are, W273
Your Witness, W274

APPENDIX B
CHRONOLOGICAL LIST OF COMPOSITIONS

Numbers following each title (e.g., W137) refer to the "Works and Performances" section of this volume.

1936   Haile Selassie, W107

1937   Allegro in E minor for piano, W82
        Serenade in G for piano, W117
        Theme and Three Variations, W326
        Three Pieces for Piano, W130

1938   Day Dreams, W85
        Grand Fantasia, W106
        Kensington Gardens, W153

1939   Two Part-Songs, W150

1940   Overture for Wind Octet, W109
        Suite Bourgeoise, W128

1941   Phantasy for String Quartet, W110
        Two Pieces for Piano, W137
        Two Sketches for Oboe and Piano, W327

1942   Divertimento [No.1] for Orchestra (Opus 1), W32
        Quintet for Wind (Opus 2), W116
        Sonata for Flute and Piano, W118
        Sonata for Piano in B minor, W120

1943   Beckus the Dandipratt (Opus 5), W12
        Double-Hoquet, W317
        Larch Tress (Opus 3), W47

Motel-Marie Assumptio, W318
Three Pieces for Piano, W131
Three Shanties for Wind Quintet (Opus 4), W132
Trio for Flute, Viola and Bassoon (Opus 6), W134

1944   Quintet for Flute, Violin, Viola, Horn and Bassoon (Opus 7), W115
Two Songs for Voice and Piano (Opus 8), W156
Variations on a Ukranian Folk Song (Opus 9), W138

1945   Concerto [No.1] for Horn and Orchestra (Opus 11), W21
Duo for Flute and Violin (Opus 10), W87
Prelude for Piano, W111
Symphonic Suite for Orchestra (Opus 12), W65

1946   Festival Overture (Opus 14), W39
Symphony for Strings (Opus 13), W66

1947   Avalanche Patrol, W163
Children's Suite for Piano (Opus 16), W83
Seven RAF Flashes, W243
Sonata for Viola and Piano (Opus 17), W121
Sonata [No.1] for Violin and Piano (Opus 15), W122
Two Bagatelles for Piano (Opus 18), W136

1948   Badgers Green, W164
Charting the Seas, W177
Concerto [No.1] for Clarinet and Strings (Opus 20), W15
Cotton-Lancashire's Time for Adventure, W180
Gates of Power, W195
Hawick, Queen of the Border, W197
Hydrography, W204
Metropolitan Water Board, W219
Mining Review, W220
Only a Little Box of Soldiers, W320
Report on Steel, W235
Smoke, The (Opus 21), W62
Sonatina for Flute and Piano (Opus 19), W125
Struggle for Oil, The, W250
To Youth, W78
Two RAF Flashes, W261
Women in Out Time, W272

1949   Anthony and Cleopatra, W162

Beautiful Country of Ayr, The, W167
Britannia Mews, W173
Dollars and Sense, W186
Drums for a Holiday, W187
EVWs, W190
Flight for a Fuller Life, W192
Frazers of Cabot Cove, The, W194
Henri Christophe, W2
Julius Caesar, W212
Quartet for Strings [No.1] (Opus 23), W113
Science of the Orchestra, W241
Symphony No.1 (Opus 22), W67
Terra Incognita, W253
This Farming Business, W255
Trieste: Problem City, W259
When you went Away, W265
Your Witness, W274

1950   Airways, W158
Divertimento [No.2] for Orchestra (Opus 24), W33
ECA Productivity Team, W189
English Dances [Set 1] (Opus 27), W34
Fifty Acres, W191
Let go for'ard, W214
Oil Review No.5, W227
Psalm 150 (Opus 25), W142
Riddle of Japan, The, W236
Serenade for Small Orchestra (Opus 26), W57
This is Britain, W256
Up for the Cup, W262
Where Britain Stands, W266

1951   Alien Orders, W160
Concerto for Piano Duet and Strings (Opus 32), W25
English Dances [Set 2] (Opus 330, W35
Home at Seven, W202
Home to Danger, W203
Local Newspapers, W216
Man and Machines, W218
No Highway, W224
Power for All, W230
Sonatina for Clarinet and Piano (Opus 29), W124
Sonatina for Oboe and Piano (Opus 28), W126

Sussex Overture (Opus 31), W64
Up at the Villa, W4
Wings of Danger, W270

1952   Channel Islands, W176
Concerto for Oboe and Strings (Opus 39), W23
Curtain Up, W182
Dancing Master, The (Opus 34), W1
Divertimento for Wind Trio (Opus 37), W86
Eight Children's Pieces for Piano (Opus 36), W90
Four-Sided Triangle, W193
Holly and the Ivy, The, W201
Invitation to the Dance, W208
Island, The, W209
It Started in Paradise, W211
Ringer, The, W237
Sound Barrier, The, W247
Stolen Face, W248
Two Ceremonial Psalms (Opus 35), W149

1953   Albert RN, W159
Captain's Paradise, The, W174
Copenhagen, City of Towers, W179
Devil on Horseback, W185
Flourish for a 21st Birthday (Opus 44), W300
Hobson's Choice, W200
Homage to the Queen (Opus 42), W6
Katherine, Walking and Running, W108
Man of Africa, W217
Powered Flight, W231
Purple Dust, W286
Sonata [No.2] for Violin and Piano (Opus 43), W123
Sonatina for Recorder and Piano (Opus 41), W127
Story of Gilbert and Sullivan, The, W249
Symphony No.2 (Opus 40), W68
Tango in D, W321
You Know What Sailors Are, W273

1954   Beautiful Stranger, W168
Belles of St. Trinian's, The, W169
Concerto for Flute and Strings (Opus 45), W17
Concerto for Harmonica and Orchestra (Opus 46), W20
Concerto for Organ and Orchestra (Opus 47), W24

Constant Husband, The, W178
Paddy's Nightmare, W284
Prize of Gold, A, W232
Rinaldo and Armida (Opus 49), W7
Royal Tour, The - New Zealand, W240
Sea Shall Not Have Them, The, W242
Sinfonietta [No.1] (Opus 48), W59
Sleeping Tiger, The, W245
Tempest, The, W288
War in the Air, W291
Welcome the Queen, W264

1955   Candlemas Night, W275
Deep Blue Sea, The, W184
Electra, W276
Fanfare for a Festival, W293
I am a Camera, W205
John Clare Cantata (Opus 52), W139
Night My Number Came Up, The, W221
1984, W223
Serenade for Guitar and Strings (Opus 50), W56
Tam O'Shanter (Opus 51), W76
Value for Money, W263
Woman for Joe, The, W271

1956   Barretts of Wimpole Street, The, W165
Concerto [No.2] for Horn and Strings (Opus 58), W22
Fanfare - ABC TV Title Music, W278
Fanfare for a Royal Occasion, W294
Grand, Grand Overture, A (Opus 57), W46
Hill in Korea, A, W199
Open Window, The (Opus 56), W3
Port Afrique, W229
Roses Tattoo, W239
Solitaire, W8
Song of Praise (Opus 55), W146
Tiger in the Smoke, W257
Trapeze, W258
Trio for Violin, Viola and Piano (Opus 54), W135
Wicked as They Come, W268

1957   Blue Murder at St. Trinian's, W170
Bridge on the River Kwai, The, W172

Commonwealth Christmas Overture (Opus 64), W14
Dunkirk, W188
For Mr Pye an   Island, W280
Four Scottish Dances (Opus 59), W43
HRH The Duke of Cambridge (Opus 60), W301
Island in the Sun, W210
Quartet for Oboe and Strings (Opus 61), W112
Richmond, W312
Royal Prologue, W287
Symphony No.3 (Opus 63), W69
Toy Symphony (Opus 62), W79

1958   Concert Piece for Percussion, W84
Coupe des Alpes, W181
Inn of the Sixth Happiness, The, W206
Key, The, W213
Roots of Heaven, The, W238
Sinfonietta [No.2] (Opus 65), W60
United Nations, W80

1959   Boy and the Bridge, The, W171
Concerto for Guitar and Chamber Orchestra (Opus 67), W19
Five William Blake Songs (Opus 66), W152
Four Pieces for Chamber Ensemble, W105
Kingston Fanfare, W303
Music for You, W283
On the Brow of Richmond Hill, W319
Solomon and Sheba, W246
Song of Simeon (Opus 69), W147
Suddenly Last Summer, W251
Sweeney Todd (Opus 68), W9

1960   Angry Silence, The, W161
Carnival of Animals (Opus 727), W13
Christmas Carol Arrangements, W316
Hoffnung Fanfare, W302
March: Overseas (Opus 70), W307
No Love for Johnnie, W225
Parasol, W285
Pure Hell of St. Trinian's, W233
Quintet for Brass (Opus 73), W309
Symphony No.4 (Opus 71), W70
Tunes of Glory, W260

1961   Grand Concerto Gastronomique (Opus 76), W45
        Leonora [Overture] No.4, W48
        On the Fiddle, W228
        Symphony No.5 (Opus 74), W71
        Whistle Down the Wind, W267

1962   Concerto for two Violins and String Orchestra (Opus 77), W30
        Inspector, The, W207
        Lion, The, W215
        Little Suite [No.2] (Opus 78), W49
        Nine Hours to Rama, W222
        We Three Kings of Orient Are, W324

1963   Chalk Garden, The, W175
        Electra (Opus 79), W75
        Espionage, W277
        Gala Performance, W281
        Little Suite [No.1] for Brass Band (Opus 80), W304
        Peacock in the Zoo, The, W141
        Tamahine, W252

1964   Five Pieces for Violin and Piano (Opus 84), W104
        Great St. Trinian's Train Robbery, The, W196
        Sinfonietta [No.3] (Opus 81), W61
        Sunshine Overture (Opus 83), W63
        Thin Red Line, The, W254
        Water Music (Opus 82), W315

1965   Duo for Two Cellos (Opus 85), W89
        Fantasy for Bassoon (Opus 86), W91
        Fantasy for Clarinet (Opus 87), W93
        Fantasy for Flute (Opus 89), W94
        Fantasy for Horn (Opus 88), W97
        Fantasy for Oboe (Opus 90), W98
        Theme for Player's, W289

1966   Africa - Texas Style, W157
        Four Cornish Dances (Opus 91), W41
        Heroes of Telemark, The, W198
        Jolly Old Friar, W140
        Sky West and Crooked, W244
        Theme and Variation, W77

1967   Little Suite [No.2] for Brass Band (Opus 95), W305
        North Sea Strike, W226
        Padstow Lifeboat, The (Opus 94), W308
        Salute to Thomas Merritt (Opus 98), W55
        Symphony No.6 (Opus 95), W72
        This Christmas Night, W148
        Thomas Merritt: Coronation March, W323
        Trevelyan Suite (Opus 96), W133
        Turtle Drum, The (Opus 92), W290

1968   Anniversary Overture (Opus 99), W11
        First Lady, The, W279
        Peterloo (Opus 97), W51
        St. Endellion Ringers, W144
        Savile Centenary Fanfare, W313
        Thomas Merritt: Anthems and Carols, W322

1969   Battle of Britain, The, W166
        Concerto for Two Pianos (3 hands) and Orchestra (Opus 104), W29
        David Copperfield, W183
        Fantasy for Trombone (Opus 101), W101
        Fantasy for Trumpet (Opus 100), W102
        Fantasy for Tuba (Opus 102), W103
        Reckoning, The, W234
        Song of Accounting Periods, The (Opus 103), W154

1970   Concerto for Twenty-Eight Players (Opus 105), W28
        Fanfare for Louis, W295
        Fantasy for Audience and Orchestra (Opus 106), W37
        Fantasy for Guitar (Opus 107), W95

1971   Concerto for Viola and Chamber Orchestra (Opus 108), W31
        Fanfare for One, 80 Years Young, W296
        William Walton: Sonata for String Orchestra, W325

1972   Concerto [No.2] for Flute and Orchestra (Opus 111), W18
        Fair Field, The (Opus 110), W36
        Popular Birthday, W53
        Song of Freedom (Opus 109), W145

1973   Fantasy for Brass Band (Opus 114a), W298
        Flourish for Orchestra (Opus 112), W40
        Symphony No.7 (Opus 113), W73

1974   Concerto [No.2] for Clarinet and Orchestra (Opus 115), W16
        Two John Donne Songs (Opus 114b), W155

1975   Fantasy for Harp (Opus 117), W96
        Fantasy on a Theme of John Field for Piano and Orchestra (Opus 116),
        W38
        Quartet for Strings [No.2] (Opus 118), W114
        Railway Fanfare, W311

1976   Philharmonic Concerto (Opus 120), W52
        Return of Odysseus, The (Opus 119), W143
        Three Musketeers, The, W10

1977   Hard Times, W282
        Sonata for Flute and Piano (Opus 121), W119
        Variations for Orchestra on a Theme of Ruth Gipps (Opus 122), W81

1978   Symphony for Brass (Opus 123), W314
        Symphony No.8 (Opus 124), W74

1980   Wildcats of St. Trinian's, The, W269

1982   Concerto for Trumpet and Orchestra (Opus 125), W27

1986   Fantasy for Recorder (Opus 127), W99
        Four Irish Dances (Opus 126), W42
        Symphony No.9 (Opus 128), W75
        Three Fantasies for Piano (Opus 129), W129

1987   Fantasy for Cello (Opus 130), W92
        Little Suite [No.3] for Brass Band (Opus 131), W306
        Quintet [No.2] for Brass (Opus 132), W310

1988   Concerto for Recorder and Orchestra (Opus 133), W26
        Contrasts (Opus 134), W151
        Divertimento for Wind Octet (Opus 137), W292
        Duo for Two B-flat Clarinets (Opus 135), W88
        Shakespearean Cello Concerto (Opus 136), W58

1989   Four Welsh Dances (Opus 138), W144

1990   Fantasy for Recorder and String Quartet (Opus 140), W100
        Flourish for a Battle (Opus 139), W299

Manx Suite, A (Opus 142), W50
Robert Kett Overture (Opus 141), W54

INDEX

Page number references refer to pages in the "Biography"; other entries refer to individual items in the "Works and Performances" list (W), the "Discography" (D) and the "Bibliography" (B).

Since the Bibliography is arranged alphabetically by author, index listings for these items have not been included under the author's name (although, of course, other references to those authors are indexed).

BBC Welsh Symphony Orchestra, W77
Bedford, Steuart, W26
Beinum, Edward van, p.4; W12
Bell, Mary Hayley, W244, W267
Bennett, Compton, W211
Berkeley, Lennox, W296
Berkley, Martin, W248
Best, Roger, W31; D19
Bettinson, Ralph, W223
Birmingham International Wind Competition, W91, W93, W94, W97, W98
Bisset, Donald, W276
Black Dyke Mills Band, W308
Blades, James, W84, W290
Blair, James, W74
Blake William, W151, W152
Blezard, William, W284
Bliss, Arthur, W296
Bloodworth, Dennis, W49, W90
B.M.C. Band, W308
Boettcher, Wilfred, W18
Boisvert, Emmanuelle, D34
Bolton, Ivor, D8, D9
Boothroyd, Derrick, W263
Boulle, Pierre, W172
Boult, Adrian, p.4; W34, W77, W300
Bourgue, Maurice, W98
Bournemouth Municipal Orchestra, W62, W68
Bournemouth Symphony Orchestra, W40; D7, D71, D78
Bowden, Pamela, W152, W319; D33
Boyd Neel Orchestra, W17, W23, W59
Bradnum, Frederick, W275
Brahms, Caryl, W285
Brain, Dennis, W22, W46, W317, W318
Brand, Geoffrey, W145
Brandenburg Concerto (J.S. Bach), B30
Brass North Ltd., W44
Bream, Julian, W19, W56, W95; D11
Brigade of Guards, W313
Briggs, Claire, D83
Brighton Philharmonic Society, W64
Brighouse, Harold, W200
British Broadcasting Corporation (BBC), W14, W20, W29, W37, W43, W70,
        W77, W285, W290, W312

About the Author

STEWART R. CRAGGS is Professor of Music Bibliography at the University of Sunderland. He is the author of a number of bio-bibliographies including *Arthur Bliss: A Bio-Bibliography* (Greenwood, 1988), *Richard Rodney Bennett: A Bio-Bibliography* (Greenwood, 1990), *John McCabe: A Bio-Bibliography* (Greenwood, 1991), *Alun Hoddinott: A Bio-Bibliography* (Greenwood, 1993), and *William Mathias: A Bio-Bibliography* (Greenwood, 1995).

Recent Titles in Bio-Bibliographies in Music

Paul Creston: A Bio-Bibliography
Monica J. Slomski, compiler

William Thomas McKinley: A Bio-Bibliography
Jeffrey S. Sposato

William Mathias: A Bio-Bibliography
Stewart R. Craggs

Carl Ruggles: A Bio-Bibliography
Jonathan D. Green

Gardner Read: A Bio-Bibliography
Mary Ann Dodd and Jayson Rod Engquist

Allen Sapp: A Bio-Bibliography
Alan Green

William Grant Still: A Bio-Bibliography
Judith Anne Still, Michael J. Dabrishus, and Carolyn L. Quin

Ross Lee Finney: A Bio-Bibliography
Susan Hayes Hitchens

Gerald Finzi: A Bio-Bibliography
John C. Dressler

Larry Sitsky: A Bio-Bibliography
Robyn Holmes, Patricia Shaw, and Peter Campbell

George Whitefield Chadwick: A Bio-Bibliography
Bill F. Faucett

William Schuman: A Bio-Bibliography
K. Gary Adams

ISBN 0-313-29254-X

90000>

EAN

9 780313 292545

HARDCOVER BAR CODE